Creative Resonance

Poetry: Elegant Play, Elegant Change

by
Ambika Talwar

Golden Matrix Visions
2006

Copyright © 2006 by Ambika Talwar. All rights reserved.

Published by Golden Matrix Visions
gmvisions@yahoo.com
http://www.preciousheartchi.com

Printed in the United States of America
First printing January 2006

10 9 8 7 6 5 4 3 2 1

Library of Congress Control Number: 2005911317

Talwar, Ambika
Creative Resonance — Poetry: Elegant Play, Elegant Change

ISBN 10: 1-59975-674-9
ISBN 13: 978-1-59975-674-5

Cover concept by Michael R. Evans ~
http://www.michaelrevans.com

Cover design and book layout by Charlie Schlafke ~
http://www.everything-artistic.com

Illustrations by Ambika Talwar

To

My students
Your light and magnificence
Dorothea Kenny and all my teachers who passed on the flame

*For Kadi
with love
Ambika
6-Nov-2014
(Purnima)*

Acknowledgements & Inspirations ~

For giving me this purpose and reason, my former students: Peter Ngo, Vu Dung, Paul Aguirre, Kathleen Duncan, Joseph (Hyung) Cho, Lisa Van Deusen, Sean Cottrel, Mario Chairez, Jason Merchey, and many many more. They inspired me to find the spaces explored within, made me review existing exercises and create new ones, and compelled me to write this book.

For both personal and creative support, my warmest gratitude to Cornelia Ballent, Shirley Saraga, John Payne, Gloria Kamler, Betsey Carpenter, Gail de Mallac, Nichole Dermody, and Johnny Seitz.

For keeping me on track and bringing me to where I want to be, my gratitude to Laara Lindo ~ poet and friend, whose light and joyfulness are a source of growth, encouragement and celebration of the finest in life; Dorothea Kenny ~ my mythology professor at CSUF, Fullerton, who knows the mythologies of the world and nine languages and would be horrified if I had a truant apostrophe; Yasuhiko Genku Kimura ~ teacher, friend, and inspiration; Vianna Stibal ~ whose teachings have been a blessing to thousands on this planet; David Hawkins ~ whose book *Power vs. Force* was an inspiration; Peter Stanlis and Joan Clark ~ whom I met because of this book and whose words resonate; David Flaten ~ friend and mentor, who is always there when I want him; Lisa Cannon ~ my coach, who gently and surely made me think bigger than I was ready for; Surender Talwar ~ my father, whose longing for beauty and simplicity is poetic and I relate; Ramma Talwar ~ my mother, who just is.

I thank also my beautiful cohorts in creation in a workshop lead by Yasuhiko Genku Kimura (Dec. 10-11, 2005): James Autio, Summer Autio, Hideo Nakajima, Carmen Alcaraz, Bud Krogh, Michael R. Evans, Linda Marcus, Kevin Rafferty, Dan Gleason, Etsuko Kimura. Their presence returns with me. Their magnificence shifts universes.

For shaking up my overuse of "And," for editorial assistance, for grounding me with things to do, and for answering my calls, my gratitude to friend and Los Angeles poet, Mani Suri.

I thank also the countless stories and philosophies told me in my childhood—they have been referred to but not referenced.

Thanks also to the limitless creative potential which helps us to see grace and beauty everywhere.

Table of Contents

Prolog ix

Part I
Chapter 1 — The Process Within 3
Chapter 2 — Recreating Relationships 15
Chapter 3 — Cultural Connections 27
Chapter 4 — Body Architectonics 41
Chapter 5 — Power of Silence 51
Chapter 6 — The Word: Our Law 57
Chapter 7 — Prayer of Gratitude 67
Chapter 8 — Being the Beloved 73
Chapter 9 — Poetry of Source Within 85
Chapter 10 — The Gift 91

Part II
Continuum: A Love Story 97

Epilog 127

Appendix 128

Glossary 131

References 132

Prolog ~

Dear Co-Creators ~

Welcome and many thanks for sharing your time and energy with me as you read my book. This book is intended for you—teachers, holistic practitioners, students of poetry and those who wish to develop a poetic vision.

My purpose in writing this book is to explore my experiences in the classroom and reveal the light and the power in each single universe (student) that exists, as it struggles to know itself. My additional purpose is to infuse our poetic consciousness into all areas of our lives. Finally, this book has been a personal journey of revelation and opening.

I have deliberately divided the book into two parts. Part I consists of ten chapters which explore my process as applicable to different areas of thought and co-creation. Each chapter follows from the previous, touching upon the various aspects of our experiences whether they be explored inside or outside a typical classroom or workshop environment. Part II consists of a short story titled "Continuum," which embodies some of the ideas contained in Part I.

This is not, nor was meant to be, an academic endeavor. It is part narrative, part explanation, part exploration, and it came about from my active participation with my universe. A universe that has been filled with joys, confusions, delusions, sorrows, laughters, and lessons– indeed, the medicines have been sometimes painful. But as the elegant strings that we are, it is through lessons that we become cleansed and strengthened. And, importantly, I was working with groups of young people whose desire for something more spoke to me.

Excited at writing about my poetic process, I went online and typed the words "poetry as revelation." To my surprise I found an address given to students of the University of Detroit in 1962 by Dr. P. J. Stanlis under the same title. Here are his words–they spoke to me utterly and completely.

"Poetry in the modern world, as always in the past, is largely concerned with revealing God, man and nature to the human race. A finished poem is capable of revealing the deepest insights into the meaning and value of the universe and ourselves. As revelation, a finished poem is so rooted in objective reality that it becomes a new thing, capable of appealing to our senses, our minds, our emotions and imaginations, in short, to our total nature. The revelation is not merely of knowledge, but of love; it involves not recognition only, but communication and response,

which is correspondence; it begins in ecstatic pleasure, and ends in calm wisdom. Between a good poem and a responsive reader there is instant rapport, pure sympatico. That is what makes poetry at once undefinable yet unmistakable. The value of poetry is like the value of a state of grace - an end in itself. Poetry for its own sake implies that our love of it should be audacious and intrinsic, unmixed by motives or interests of practical utility, or the dilettantish knowledge of the culture vulture."

Indeed, a Robert Frost friend and scholar, Dr. Stanlis could not have already said as eloquently what is the theme of my rambling rose. Curious to connect with him, I found a contact online for Friends of Robert Frost in Vermont. A lady there gave me his number. I recall coming away from my conversation with Dr. Stanlis tingling with excitement–I felt magnificent.

Such poetic moments cleanse us of grime, taking us to our greater self, demanding that we be aware, attentive, awake, and alive at all times. It is often through our imagination that we find a way out of the dilemmas imposed on us through culture and control. The Romantics knew well that the Imagination was the path to an ideal world. I like to call the process and effect of active engagement with our imagination: a transcendence of the fusion of all our senses which, filtered and transformed, leads to a recreation of a grander world of possibilities and self-awareness.

I am reminded of my visit to the Pinon Mountains for the historic Mars viewing in August 2003. The sky so full with stars was breathtakingly beautiful. Looking at the grand magnificence, I squinted. That made all the stars seem connected with lines that twinkled from one star to the other. The sky transformed into an interconnected network. When I looked without squinting, the stars shone like separate entities. It became a lovely game. I asked a physicist why that happened. He noted that it is the imagination that connects them–a poetic explanation, indeed, for a phenomenon of physics and optics and *apropos* for my moment of play.

Truly, it was a profound and complete moment. Such moments remind us that our elegant filaments, our living strings, are in place at all times. We, in our poetic recognition, are in resonance at all times whether it be in joy or not. Why not be in joy?

Playing with the night sky made me realize that the work I had been doing with the poetic process was designed to bring the whole person in touch with their authentic self–integrating mind, body, and spirit. I call my work and process *Creative Resonance*. It has become my mission.

Creative Resonance™ is a singular process that I developed combining principles of polarity therapy, further elaborated in the book, and the creative process. With experience as a poet, artist, filmmaker, as well as a holistic practitioner, it became clear to me that language was and is the prime mover and motivator of our reality. That reality may be in health or its lack, of love or its lack, of joy or its lack, of self-confidence or its lack, et al. Moreover, we understand from various holistic techniques that what we experience resides in our tissue and cellular memory–thus our resonance factor may change as we grow in experience for our memory thus also expands and becomes more compact–this does not mean that we remember everything that we experience. Sometimes, as a result of this experiencing through thought, word, action, and external stimuli of various kinds, we may become out of balance with our own sense of what is right and true for our integrity. This is where Creative Resonance comes in.

A selective combination of polarity processes–focusing, recognizing and identifying the experience in the body, and allowing it to express itself so that it can be changed and rearranged–assists in revealing to us when we are not in synch and how to regain balance. We can change how we receive an experience so that we resonate more closely with our core integrity. This is the process of Creative Resonance. I use creative writing or movement or visualization to initiate a release and then recreate the experience with a fresh understanding. This allows practitioner and client to own and be empowered–this renewed being then is a sensed and felt experience grounded in inner knowing. In the classroom, the process is a little different.

Creative Resonance is a process that I employ in many ways both in holistic workshops and in the classroom. It is simple, effective, and powerful.

In loving gratitude to all of you who make these thoughts and me possible.

Ambika Talwar

Surrender to light,
where rainbow strings make music.
Walk into my eyes.
~ Ambika Talwar

Part I

Chapter 1 ~ The Process Within

The poet, as everyone knows, must strike his individual note sometime between the ages of fifteen and twenty-five. He may hold it a long time, or a short time, but it is then that he must strike it or never. School and college have been conducted with the almost express purpose of keeping him busy with something else till the danger of his ever creating anything is past.
     ~ Robert Frost

Several pairs of eyes are on me—some droopy, some eager, some in the in-between place. Starting a new lesson, I take a deep breath and enter their varied worlds with the following: *Poetry is a revelatory experience that transports you to a place outside of your self where you find you. So, in reading a poem, you enter the world that the poem creates for you, and once you are in that world, you begin to find yourself. And even if reading a poem is a challenge (because poetry can be sometimes obtuse) and doing so throws you into an experience of a still point, be with it because that is precisely what will induce in you a trance through which you are transported to a world of which you knew nothing at all—but one in which you will find your Self. When you suddenly find that other world, it fills you with the power and excitement as though of a revelation. And it truly is one, for in that space you have suddenly come face to face with that which really matters, that which is alive and vital, that which is indestructible, and which is the very thing which gets consumed in the dross of our daily existence, and we get lost, frustrated, tired, angry, disappointed.*

This is usually the essence of what I tell my students in a literature class when I introduce the poetry genre mid-semester.

So we read Audre Lorde's "Coping," a brief free verse poem in which we see small islands and puddles created after a rainfall. A small boy spoons out water from a puddle so that seeds that have not fed on sunlight can experience it and survive. Who would think that spooning water out of a puddle would free the spirit of the reader? But this tiny moment is so focused and so complete not only for the boy in the act of spooning out water, but for the reader who enters the space of the experience, which thereby expands the reader's own world to include that of the boy, that the reader then must find that same tendency in him/herself–the tendency of relating to the act of spooning out the water with intent. The reader, too, lives that experience and can own it. In the reader then is revealed a hieratic mystery—the interconnectedness of us all. This the ancients had known; therefore, it is no wonder that their early writings were in poetic form–a form that is precise and economical so that no word or image be lost or meaning be obfuscated by too much rendering.

I suggest that poetry is a revelation of both our inner and outer worlds—sometimes, of course, there is no difference. And in the experiencing of the poetic, a continuum, we are thrown into that mystery that so carefully hides as we run hither and thither in complete distraction and disarray performing our responsibilities that bring us the dough, that throw us into the wilderness of weaknesses and dilemmas competing for attention so that we truly get lost in the maze. We lack time or the inclination to delve into the poetic and, thereby, retrieve ourselves.

So I looked at my students who were waiting and wondering about what I would say next. After having driven 40 miles to campus, taught 75 minutes in an argumentation class and almost two hours in a composition class, held one hour in my office, I had expended enough energy and so wanted to go back home. But I had this class at 12:30 p.m., and I had to fulfill my duty to them as well. I felt tired and did not feel ready to open the big thick heavy black book titled *Discovering Literature* (ed. 2002). I wondered whether they wondered if I was just tired, or whether I was prepared to teach their class that day. Hmmm, and then I had become disillusioned with the bookish way of teaching poetry, whereby we explain that "meaning in poetry is conveyed through images and sounds.... Metaphor is...." We then ask the class to share examples, brainstorm ideas, and share their interpretations. Initially there might be an awkward silence, then someone nervously ventures an answer and we discuss literary devices. We had already covered the meaning of metaphor in the early part of the semester when we read and discussed short stories. So what next? I asked them to turn to the page that explored various definitions with examples from poems. They did.

Then I thought, "what next?" Surely, this is not poetry. Surely, something vital is missing from our classes. Surely, this is not real learning and education. How could I take them through the exercise of finding the poetic in the poems–in their lives? In other words, of being conscious of a heightened sense of being. I decided to stay with Lorde's "Coping"–ironic that the title itself mirrored what I was doing in order to move into another space of knowing and explaining the poem.

So we read Lorde's poem again. I reminded them that the most ordinary things are complete universes and that when we look at them, really look at them, we know them. We must, of course, take the time away from unnecessary details in life, and use our time to recognize the mundane and ordinary in its extra-ordinary aspect. I realized for the first time that I could probably spend an entire hour on just a few lines. I laughed at myself, for my tendency had been to race through too much text, for I wanted them to know more poems. Of course, I had shared in my previous classes such explorations of the poetic, but I hadn't stopped so frequently nor slowed as much as I did this time. I remembered Tom Wayman's poem "Unemployed" in which he compares the person waiting in line to a postage stamp, waiting to be useful.

    This waiting in time for space to fill with something made me realize how important it was to enjoy this lesson, this chapter in suspended time, and to not hurry. Then William Wordsworth's poem came to mind–it follows below.

I Wandered Lonely as a Cloud

I WANDERED lonely as a cloud
That floats on high o'er vales and hills,
When all at once I saw a crowd,
A host, of golden daffodils;
Beside the lake, beneath the trees,
Fluttering and dancing in the breeze.

Continuous as the stars that shine
And twinkle on the milky way,
They stretched in never-ending line
Along the margin of a bay: 10
Ten thousand saw I at a glance,
Tossing their heads in sprightly dance.

The waves beside them danced; but they
Out-did the sparkling waves in glee:
A poet could not but be gay,
In such a jocund company:
I gazed—and gazed—but little thought
What wealth the show to me had brought:

For oft, when on my couch I lie
In vacant or in pensive mood,   20
They flash upon that inward eye
Which is the bliss of solitude;
And then my heart with pleasure fills,
And dances with the daffodils.

(http://www.bartleby.com/145/ww260.html)

I also recalled my short poem towards the end of my manuscript titled *Still Point—Journeys in Unwinding*, poems about my experience with the polarity process as other participants and I explored the stories in us. All this in the space of a few seconds.

XXX.

And then I know
I am a circuit of lines
of force
Prana
Chi
Ruah

waiting to lift
the geometry of my body

to the deep tonal lilt
of the duduk
to the dream drone
of the didgeridoo
to the satin baroque
of the harp
to the ancient sounds
of the mantras
that speak to my many
circles of sound vortices.

the body is the temple
of sacred proportions.

My mind wandered and I hesitated, uncertain as to what to do next. I looked at each of them. Several students had not shown up since a paper was due that very class period. I remained silent, having no desire to speak. I think I was in a moment of chaos in my mind and body, allowing for the confusion of how to proceed to settle into some order, some harmony. When this precognitive confusion finds its balance in the body, intelligence has taken over. Then the solution can become clear if we just allow the dynamic to find its space. A lesson unfolds in the mind and then I know how best to proceed. But until such a moment, I was in a deep silence. I had lost touch with the ability to speak.

Such a moment of confusion may be explained as a still point, which is a moment of chaos in the consciousness of the body. This chaos is stillness and this stillness is chaos as the body figures out how and where to move energy. The still point is a critical moment in the polarity process, a holistic practice, wherein the client (receiving a session) has found the place of balance in his/her consciousness and that of the body. When suddenly things fall in place and energy flows in a happier way, one tends to register it in different ways—one may be to let out a long deep breath signifying recognition and understanding. The body has found its place of harmony. This silence then is restful.

Of course, not everyone loses touch with language at that point—I do. I have a history of it–of being in a silenced mode in reaction to cultural strictures. Now when I lose my voice, I feel a sense of liberation. I feel at complete rest with the world. I feel infused. Words, too many words, are noise.

But poetry is expansion, sometimes in its silence.

A Continuing Dialogue

So I turned back to "Coping" (which is probably what I was doing at that time and this recognition makes me now laugh at the synchronicity of it all) I, too, was coping. And that means that so were my kids. Coping with the book, with me, with their lives, their responsibilities.

Reflecting on the poem, I noted that good poetry must be economical, precise. I asked them to avoid writing hallmark card poems, which tend to drip with syrupy sweetness. Of course, there is room for sentimentality in poetry, but it must be expressed in such a way that one may experience the tenderness and not be cloyed by it. One wants to be elevated by it and not have to swallow saccharine. They looked at me. I continued, remarking on the richness and depth of the poem "Coping."

I wanted them to know that the image is "the vehicle of emotion." Now all this is a fairly intellectual idea–good old poet T.S. Eliot always comes to my aid. How are they to understand this process? Feel it? Experience it? Know it? "It takes you into this other world beyond your self in which you find your self." It all sounds very good. But what of it? I wanted them to experience the moment of finding that connection with the subject of a particular poem that reveals itself so fully so that they could understand (or know) it for themselves. The act of knowing the poetic experience is also empowering.

So I started with association exercises. My next step was to use postures to project images and thereby evoke emotion. I would prompt with key words. For instance, I allowed my hands to droop one over the other and to wear a pensive air. I asked them to give me images that popped into their minds that reflected my posture. They said, "sad," "gloomy," and other such words. I prompted them to develop similes in order to push the description further. I suggested the idea of a widow wrapped in her sorrow, her hands falling purposelessly like lace. They liked that.

Then I called out words and had them develop images to convey the emotion. Love or joy or sadness or anger. I wanted them to get away from clichés–not just say "raging anger" but also convey that emotion with a powerful distinct image. Perhaps from nature or the kitchen. Something like "a can of hot peppers burst from the seams and his eyes bulged." I wanted them to go all out with this. Truly, we had a wonderful time playing. For it is, after all, play. Play does not connote lack of struggle.

The power of the image was made manifest–they were getting it.

It was time to return to "Coping"–to its unique world and perspective—the boy spooning out the water to give the seeds an opportunity to grow instead of dying; now the students each also realized the gentle power of small acts. They came in touch with their compassionate selves. They grew in other ways. The class had filled with a wonderful presence—that was the presence in each that had come out of hiding. Je— and Ke— both had tears in their eyes. I asked Je— to explain what she had experienced. Finding that she was stuck for words (lose touch with the ability to speak up and aloud), I turned around and suggested that they instead write down their storm as they were experiencing it. That surely would have been of more value to them. So they did.

There is no way to measure these moments, but to feel them, to know them. And they had learned that poetry takes us to another place beyond ourselves wherein we find ourselves. They had learned that the image is the "vehicle of emotion." They had learned that the ordinary things often remind us of that which is most extraordinary. They had learned that they each have the power to travel, as John Keats noted in "Ode to a Nightingale," on the "viewless wings of poesy."

The Poem Goes On In the Mind

When we met in class two days later, I asked, "So, what is poetry?" Je— raised her hand and spoke. "Poetry is what takes us to another place beyond ourselves where we find ourselves," she noted. Her eyes were shining. What more could I say? I wondered where she had traveled.

We then proceeded to discuss and experience collectively some of the poems they had read at home. The reading list included Dylan Thomas's "Fern Hill." One of the guys raised his hand and grinned, saying, "I just don't get it." "Hmm, okay, what's confusing you?" I asked, hoping that the question might trigger something that might make him get a part even if not the whole. "Well, the whole thing, I just don't understand what he's saying," he replied. I sighed, wondering if I really wanted to explain Thomas in the middle of the already planned lesson. "Do Not Go Gentle Into That Good Night" could be rather abstruse and open to interpretation. "Fern Hill" is a much longer poem. But here was my challenge. I asked them to sit and just listen, that I'd read it aloud to them. So I did.

Then something strange and wonderful happened. The room became hushed and still. This noumena seeped into my very bones. They—my students, not my bones— were excited in a quiet sort of way. When I finished reading the poem, I asked what they felt about it. They were transfigured; they'd gotten it. They said they had understood the poem and did not need any explanation. Oh, I thought, this was easy. The power of the spoken word, the power of listening, the word given voice, the vehicle to another world–one's own world. The students got it, loved it–in other words, they received the poem and made it theirs.

They experienced the poem while I read it aloud to them. Now, of course, I felt compelled to recover some of the choice images in the poem, the color "green." The freshness of it, the playfulness of the images, the serenity—I welcome the power of association and recollection. I welcome the power of reconnection with one's own experience of childhood and of the dreams of that powerful stage in our lives. This must be what Thomas must have wanted us to know. Because we have a shared experience of childhood, or at least an idealization of it. It is no wonder that the marvelous kids in class got this easily when I read the poem aloud to them. What was important was to tell them that they were traveling to another world to find theirs.

In the words of Dylan Thomas himself, "You can tear a poem apart to see what makes it tick… You're back with the mystery of having been moved by words. The best craftsmanship always leaves holes and gaps… so that something that is not in the poem can creep, crawl, flash or thunder in."

I told my students that poets don't decide that they will use such and such metaphor or simile, personification or metonymy, pathetic fallacy or hyperbole. That it is all part of the creating of the poem. The poet does not stop and say, "I must use a metaphysical conceit now…." The poem flows through and in the re-writing, the poet may make choices to revise clichés. However, poetic thinking itself is metaphoric and the writer thus writes. It is critics who analyze the literary merits of a poem and make decisions on whose poetry is worthy of their attention.

The point of all of this is that I wanted my students to have first a felt experience of the poem—if not exactly as the poet experienced it (for that is not possible to replicate accurately) but to experience what the poet was attempting to convey and embody it. Then later they could recognize and understand the literary elements to add to their appreciation of the work. For them to understand the poetic process is far more important as I see it—for when we have touched them in these various ways, then we have also empowered them. Ourselves, too.

❖❖❖

This discussion on the poetic process, of course, led to their next big assignment.

I asked them to go to the canyon in the wee hours of dawn. They said, "what?" Nonchalantly, I said, "Yes, I want you to wake up really early one of these weekends, drive to the canyon and be there all by yourself. I want you to breathe the air, experience the changing light, breathe in the smells. I want you to listen to the birds, the ants, the leaves as they stir with the changing light. I want you to listen to your breathing, your footfall, the dust beneath your feet. I want you to feel all these things and just know something. Write about it. Bring it to class." They looked at me with jaws dropped to their knees, disbelieving smiles adding to their, "You don't really mean this, do you?" "I do," I said very firmly. What if I can't get up early? I shrugged. What if I don't do it? You'll be a bad loser. They knew I was joking with them, but not about the assignment. To all their objections, I provided simple solutions. "It's my job," I told them, "to make you do things differently.... what is more, I get paid for it."

So they did visit a canyon of their choice. My student, Paul Aguirre came to class excited and transformed–he had experienced the waking up of his inner silence. This was the first time he had seen a sunrise and he was "totally blown" by the experience. In "Awakened," he described in minute detail the transition from pre-dawn to dawn. He spoke of being "magically suspended in time," of the "shy sun hid[ing] *sic* from the moon." He spoke of the pre-dawn mist as "this white wonderland of dreams/ [that] take shape outside the inner world...." He spoke of colors and sounds with amazing vividness. He called his canyon journey, "this mysterious quest of enlightenment—not bound in a house of worship." And he wished, "To be an eagle floating on nature's breath.... /to fly high into the heavens...." but that he is "a small, insignificant/ant painted on this enormous canvas...."

Despite a tiny note of pessimism, I see this poem as another victory. This experience may have changed his life and perspective. Other students must have had a similar effect, for this invitation to find themselves in a transcendent process worked—they entered a different world without even realizing it. Coming out of it reminded them of their own richness, their uniqueness, and an opportunity to be authentic.

Generally, most students dread poetry. But here were my 18 to 35-year-olds who started to enjoy themselves very much and I was gratified. Poetry, out of reach and abstruse, had become an experience they could own. I wanted them to experience the process directly so they could make it theirs, so their lives were touched by the poetry within them. It worked. They had a new relationship with the genre–I believe they still do.

Exercises ~

1. Early morning canyon visit.

This is as described above. One may adjust the location to suit one's environments. Go to a canyon, a beach or a desert—anywhere away from an urban sprawl. The important thing is to go at the crack of dawn to experience a waking up of awareness within and the silence in the inner sanctum.

2. Name poem.

We all have a relationship with our names. Try to be someone else for a day or a few hours. Adopt a new name, a foreign name perhaps. Explore the experience of being someone else, of wearing a different persona. This is another way to be in a different place and find oneself. Details particularly make this assignment interesting and challenging, for always the learning is about oneself, one's awareness, et al.

3. Doing an activity differently or in a different environment.

When we are taken out of familiar environments, we find aspects of ourselves we would not have ordinarily done. This is a terrific exercise to break old patterns and develop new paradigms of thinking as one learns to resonate in a different way. Pick an activity that you have enjoyed. Now find a way to do it very differently from the set pattern or behavior or style. For instance, you could take a new route to school or to work so you wake up to the drive which you would otherwise have done in a trance. Or take any activity out of context and do it in another location. Note what comes up for you—what do you learn about yourself or about the activity itself? Remember that any activity is play, so think of what this game brings to your consciousness about life and its innuendoes.

Chapter 2. Recreating Relationships

Poetry is the opening and closing of a door, leaving those who look through to guess about what is seen during the moment.
  ~ Carl Sandburg

Everything, I tell my eager stalwarts, is about relationships. How we sit or stand, what cars we drive, what clothes we wear, what books we read, how we use things, what foods we eat. We are always in relationship with something or the other. We are always relating; hence, it is important to become aware of the interconnections that exist but also those that we constantly create. For, of course, we are co-creators of the drama of life–this co-creating of our relating is also our poetry.

Our life experience begins in the womb, where we are submerged in waters, not of forgetting (like the River Styx after death) but of memory. We swirl in these waters for 10 long moon months being subject to the mother's moods, experiences and dramas, including what she eats, drinks and makes merry with. Our bodybeing, as it were, is already coiled with sensations and impressions. Like flecks of gold that light our dark waters full of sounds, tastes, and smells. And right in there begins our relationship with ourselves. It is no wonder then that we usually find the sound of the heartbeat comforting and, sometimes, disconcerting. Mickey Hart's CD titled *Music to be Born By* of the heart beat can at times be soothing, and, at times, annoying. He made it to assist in the delivery of his child, for whom the transition might be more comforting.

In our transitions is also our poetry–a journey in remembering, recounting, and recreating our relationships—the foremost being the one with our Self. This process of healing, renewing, and empowering affects one right at the cellular level, and this renewing affects our relating as well. My experiences with holistic healing practices, particularly polarity principles, help to explain this effect.

One of the primary principles of polarity therapy or consciousness is that our cells contain the memory of everything that we experience. This idea of cellular memory is, of course, commonly known among holists in areas of art, science, and healing. Our cells are not only the repositories of memory of prior experience, before birth, but also of everything that we think or do or say. We are constantly being layered with new impressions. This, thereby, affects all our subsequent relating. Thus, what we create as artists then must come from a deeper source than we may realize. That which we are is already embodied in us, and that which we create is only an external manifestation of that which is constantly being related with and upon inside of us.

If the above is true, then we can say that all our stories reside in us. As a student and practitioner of polarity therapy, I can say that some of the most dramatic and revealing narratives that I have encountered or expressed have been in relationship with other polarity practitioners, specially in the space of a session whether as a practitioner or as a receiver. A session itself is a relating on different levels and with the elements—earth, water, fire, air, and ether. One leaves with a different awareness of one's own body and the things around one, as one co-creates a new relationship with people and with the environments.

When I was taking classes in polarity therapy, I found that when I returned after a class, I could not relate to foods in my refrigerator. They looked and felt different—they had a sheen or pallor that I had not noticed before. I was not drawn to eating them. While my relationship with a part of me changed, it affected my perception of the foods in my fridge as well. This is a common experience among several students of holistic healing arts—our sensitivities become more intense as our awareness expands. We become more aware of a plethora of stories in us, and there are several around food.

This relationship with food takes me to our relating with our senses, most directly to the sense of smell. I have had an aversion to the smell of milk since I was a teenager. There must be a story to explain why this happened and when. Perhaps, it was because my mother was ill and couldn't nurse me, perhaps that drinking milk seemed to be a punishment, or perhaps, very simply, that the bacteria in dairy and I were, still are, not compatible. I haven't explored the cause of this relationship fully. Maybe, it does not matter, but the polarity experience offered tools to reveal such information. The point of it is to reflect on the relationship with our past environments, how they change and affect our interactions and inter-reactions. Therefore, as a way to enhance the learning process, I bring lessons from holistic practices into the classroom. It is most important to also have fun with the unfolding dramas, while adding new thought to our changing paradigms.

Since we have a relationship with various things, I asked my students to brainstorm and explore what they learn about themselves from writing about an object from their house or even about their choice of clothes–for these tell us stories. Some years ago, my creative writing students were asked to bring to class a photo or some item for which they have a sentimental attachment. They then were to look at it, study it, know it, and write details that described it visually, then details that described its textures, what sounds they could "see-hear" in the image or object, and all the smells that came packaged with the article in question. Basically, I wanted them to heighten their awareness of their relationship with the chosen item. This, I believed, would sharpen their perception of their worlds and their place in it.

So they brought items like photos, gifts with sentimental value—anything that was special to them. They free-associated and described the item per the senses. Once they had the details down, I asked them to free associate and look for a theme that emerged from the details. They then wrote a piece creating something entirely different but using the same descriptors as listed from the prior exercise of brainstorming or getting to know the item. Amazing stories happened. Some discoveries as well.

By now, they had gotten that the thing is more than the thing itself. It is layers of emotions, layers of stories, layers of expectations and interpretations.

This is where the process can go two ways. Either way also impacts the other. One way is to just create a story and be done with it. The other way is to realize the deeper significance of the story. Either way is okay. The message chooses the medium or story and the creator or channel. The creator chooses the message and becomes the medium. The poem or narrative follows. The healing or the awareness can happen at different levels for different people. It depends on what is at that moment of greater importance and what moves the inner being to emerge. What speaks the *aha!* must walk through the door.

So it did, as in this following example in which the students explored a place beyond themselves and, in doing so, found treasures. In the fall of 1997, I gave my multicultural literature students an assignment requiring them to take one single grape or section of an orange into their mouth and to close their eyes and eat it slowly, savoring the juices, the textures, the tastes, the smells. An older Vietnamese gentleman wrote the following poem. I am proudly profoundly moved by the dignity of his work.

Nectarine
by Peter P. Ngo

I call you "my nectarine,"
A California's fruit you pick in your garden,
One early morning of spring.
Your lips reflect the reddish skin
Of my sweet nectarine.
    I recall the Vietnamese fairy tale.
    Two romantic guys wandered into the paradise.

And the fairy ladies offered the fairy peach
To make Luu, Nguyen lose their way home.

Now, in California, warm weather and blue sky
We have me again
After twenty two separated years,
You give me the late nectarine.
Oh! My lovely nectarine having a smooth, waxy skin
I have a desire for a gentle kiss
on your lip,
and a suck at a sweet, little sour
on my tongue.
I feel the drink of the God
penetrating into my blood.
So I always have you in my life
My nectarine, my lovely wife.

(First printed in *Return to Sacred Waters*, 1997. Reprinted by permission of author.)

What an amazing celebration of love from a single bite of the fruit—a recognition of the universal transcendent ideal that we are all made of the same divine stuff and experience it right here in the material body.

From student Vu Dung is this simple act of knowing the self by surrendering to anOther universe. In his poem "The Orange," he wrote that when he took the first bite, he "...forgot where I was/ It was sweet.../ That I can feel it deep down in side my veins. /Stay for a while/ I feel the whole world inside me." Surely, this is a way of knowing the self, of relating differently from what we are taught. Perhaps, we can do this process with different things so that we become clearer about our own place in the world.

The poetic experience, thus, is a revealing of relationships, or relatedness that delves deeper into the recesses of the body's imagination to bring forth something special, something unique to and about the person who is the diver into the subject (be it a photo or an object and one's relationships with it). The story or the poem must be embellished with sensory details—that is how it comes alive and invites the participation of the readers. The reader or audience furthers the relationship by experiencing the piece and being affected by it, by relating to and with it. This is a never-ending story. The poem goes on in one's mind as does the healing, the revealing, and the expansion of one's awareness.

During one class meeting, I wondered how I would make this idea of all our relatedness more real to my kids. So we discussed their choice of cars—the need for speed and the need to look cool; the clothes they like to combine—this focus on black clothes; and the foods they eat. This last raised some concerns. Some noted—"Oh! But mom doesn't cook." So what do you do? "Burger King... microwave..." "I'm poor...can't eat...." Such disclosures are hard to hear, so there was a pregnant silence wherein some shrugged their eyebrows, some smiled, and then they all looked at me waiting for the next thing. Challenge! Challenge!

Of course, I had my hands clasped together in that self-reflective stance. I said we were going to do an exercise. I had no idea where we would go with this; I also realized it was completely out of bounds as an academic exercise for it certainly did not fit into the "normal" way of teaching poetry. But then normalcy is not always my way. I could have played it safe and gone straight to the book sitting there on the table waiting to be touched. But no, I was going to dare all and touch something else. Something they would not have experienced in a college classroom.

So I took a chance and indulged in my fantasies—a fine way of finding the self in new and different situations. How else could they enter Wordsworth's world of dancing daffodils! Or the world of the boy spooning out water from the puddle where seeds would drown never to see or know the light! How else could they themselves come out to breathe and know the light! I decided to take a risk. Non-academic risk. A self-help workshop method in an academic setting. My heart pounded–what if someone snitched and said, "SHE," pointing at me "is weird." *AHA!*

Some thrill egged me on—I asked them to turn to a partner. I requested that they look deeply into each other's eyes and enter that world which is available and that which opens to them if they remain with it. It would open to them as far as they wished to travel. It is a subjective experience after all, one in which subject and object dissolve to gain a unity, where "I" and "Thou" are one, and once you have discovered it, you return to your separate selves to write–hence, know it. We rarely look each other in the eyes; we rarely make intimate contact in this way. Some cultures consider such a stare to be disrespectful— but this was not a stare. I asked them to breathe deeply as they came to know the person. Not only to take in the details but also to go into the other's eyes, where once we make contact and allow it to deepen, resistance slowly slips away.

After a momentary shyness at this unusual request, they turned to one another. They looked into each other's eyes. The guys felt conditionally awkward at being paired with a guy, but I encouraged it for I wanted them to go beyond their culturally imposed limitations.

After a few moments they settled in as well. When I asked them to return, I noticed that they had softened—I think that the experience had mellowed them into themselves.

I then asked them to speak about what they had seen and discovered. The rule was not to speak about each other in the third person as though it were a report, but to tell it to each other. So they had to use "I" and "you" instead of reporting to me in the third person. That, too, was a challenge. I realized that some things they said were projections and that was okay, for sometimes our projection is a mirrored response to the other. So while a projection is seen as transference, it may also be an interrelated reflection of aspects in the other. Jo—, one of the young stalwarts, noted that his partner, Mo— reminded him of a snake, how Mo— eyes darted quickly here and there. Mo—, on the other hand, was marked by Jo—'s calmness. I suggested that perhaps Jo—'s calmness made Mo— feel not so calm. Moreover, in this focused moment, Jo— had gone from sensing to seeing pictures, which had given him a metaphor or simile for a kind of movement, whose mood he had witnessed in Mo—. Now from here, he could create something else.

My next step was to ask them to transfer what they had seen or experienced into a metaphor. For an example, I told them that I'd seen Maja- in her innocence and sweetness, that as I looked into her dark sparkling eyes and soft rounded face, I'd been taken inwards to a place, which felt surrounded by "white clouds outlined with iridescent blue and gold." I also saw that she would become a powerful woman, grounded in her authenticity, a quality to be of service with conviction and gentleness. That her quiet grace would always be her guide–as the silent flight of swans.

It is no untruth, but of course a cliché, that eyes are the windows to the soul. We can discover new old worlds in each other's eyes each time we look into them. I mean really look. Pay attention. Be aware. This exercise had already transported them to another place. My journey with them had changed directions, and I was not sure how we would move, but I was ready to go. I knew something would be different. Perhaps, that I could open to a new challenge.

After a few moments, I brought all our attention together, to the center. Then I asked them what they had seen and how they felt. They were moved, they had traveled far to a place they had not encountered before. I knew they had met with something or someone special. I then asked them to share with the class what they had learned about the other person. This was incredible. Each had found qualities in the other they had not known before, nor could have since they only met in the space of this class. They found small special moments in that short time. Interestingly, they also found that they projected onto the other person some of their own attributes. We discovered all this in the ensuing discussion.

This exercise revealed to us the subtleties in our relating and, most importantly, I reminded my students of the power of paying attention. It is when they really paid attention to each other, that they learned who the other was, and they also learned about themselves. It also revealed the ability we have to pay attention and how easily we lose it. If only we could harness this quality in ourselves and make it a habit, then not only could we get to know one another better, but we could also realize the poetry in our connections and in our relating with each other.

This exercise reminded me of a photograph I had taken years ago in Calcutta, India, of a street child sitting on the ground making mud pies. How content he was! How complete was his universe in that moment, or string of moments! The clump of dirt had his full attention. Nothing could take that joy away. I stood and watched this child for many minutes, so moved was I at this simple and complete universe. Everything we do must command undiluted focus.

This too. The exercise of really getting to know their subject—the nectarine or peach or sliver of orange—by paying attention, by entering its universe, by relating fully made sense to them. This time it was another human being. I decided to share what I learned about Maja—. It was her utterly sweet innocence, her childlike nature that moved me so that I had to hold back my tears.

However, then came the difference in language and perception. When I shared what I had learned about Maja—, her sister protested noting that "innocence" was not right. I had to explain that it did not suggest ignorance or simplemindedness, but a simplicity that is actually most profound. She was not convinced.

Discoveries such as these made the class so much more enjoyable, so much more intense, and for many students, a road to poetry they had not imagined or fathomed opened up. Thankfully, poetry was no longer a hallmark card or something "I can't understand." It had become a journey into the language of the poet—into the relationships that a poet holds dear and that move him/her to transcend the limits of his/her own nature.

Such an experience can be grasped in every moment. There is no theory; what happens is what must. A new meaning, a new relationship is revealed to the students. And this with a new understanding of their own interconnectedness—the knowing of their ability to see better and more clearly each other, the connecting, the opening, the revealing, the interconnecting, their own innate power. Integrating one's own inner power is so necessary if we—collective humanity—are to survive, live fully, co-create, and co-evolve.

As a nectarine becomes a symbol of the poet's love and of his wife, we can each become symbols to one another of that which represents our greatest intelligence. The potential for love, compassion, and forgiveness is that intelligence. The power of integrity and joy is that intelligence. The power to create beauty is that intelligence. The power to renew and revitalize our surroundings is that intelligence. The power to be fully transformed is that intelligence. The power to simply be is our joy—and our intelligence. Thus must evolve a new relating or relatedness.

Following is an excerpt from my manuscript titled *Still Point: Journeys in Unwinding*. These excerpts reveal to me how much information is stored in our bodies and how we may be enriched by it–made wiser. This collection is based on my experiences with polarity therapy of which more is explained in Chapter 4.

VIII.

Older sisters
are clan priestesses
They teach us that
the passage to dying
is long, hard, intricate

We get lost in shadows
caught in barks of trees
We get lost on roads
that go in many directions
We get lost in garments
that wear many faces

They say that our desires
keep us wrapped in symbols
We can become what we fear
We can become what we abhor
We can become lost to ourselves
We can become the one we love

They say that the secret
to golden valleys
is beyond the glyph or the alphabet
or even through it
I ask if the desire for death
is a desire to be one with that secret

They smile. They do not reply.
But they say that the path
to the edge of golden valleys
can be silver blue

They add that when the mother leaves
the children will follow.

XVII.

      I sp
     spi spir
     it shakti
     soul am
       god
    cer
   reb
  bro
 spi
 nal
  flu
  lui
  uid
 is
it
  .
I
   circulate until the end of time in the waters of heaven and earth
   I navigate you through your memories of stories, desires, deaths
   I can be your lodestone, your fixed north star, or your boatman

    Each moment can be a revelation. Each old story can reveal a new message as one sheds limitations imposed by cultures and religions for a new paradigm. We do not have to cross into another dimension in order to find it—but we must in the here and now.

♦❖♦

Exercises ~

1. Looking into the eyes of another.

This is explained above. It provides challenges for various emotions or narratives may be evoked. And one must be ready to explore those–there might be the issue of disclosure, so it is important to establish that there be the utmost respect for each other's space.

2. Object poem.

As a student or participant, you are asked to hold an object of your choosing in your hands for a few minutes, close your eyes, and record your thoughts and sensations. Then you write a poem based on this understanding and relatedness.

In an alternative process, you may explore the object through the different senses and write your new understanding of the object. Then you use these descriptors to write about a completely different experience. In other words, you create something entirely new from the same descriptive words. We have had enormous fun with this exercise in several classes–it works well also as a process on descriptive writing. It brings you to a kinaesthetic understanding of your experience.

3. Fruit poem.

Most people are in a hurry and gobble their food. For this exercise, I ask you to take one single grape or orange section or a nectarine and look at it, hold it, be in relation with the fruit, dialogue silently–breathe it in. Then write a poem about your renewed understanding. If you then choose to take a bite, savor it for a few moments–understand it, know it. Sometimes, the result is epiphanic.

4. Breathing poem.

Sit in silence, eyes closed and breathe slowly and deeply into different parts of the body. Then maybe focus on one part and allow feelings, sensations, thoughts to come through in relation to your breathing. This experience often leads to release and renewal as patterns and paradigms are revealed.

My consideration is that after you write a poem about pain, you might transmute it into a transcendent experience of the same. As in what does the pain suggest? How can you universalize pain and suffering so that the poem you write is about humanity and not just your self? You are humanity.

This way, you can also find a new ideal to work with and be with, and you have changed your reality or perception of it. Explore what is the healing from this process for you and for humanity.

Chapter 3 ~ Cultural Connections

Poetry is the synthesis of hyacinths and biscuits.
  ~ Carl Sandburg

     Poetry takes us deep into the culture of human origins and returns us to the space prescribed and informed by our individual ethnic and/or traditional cultures. In other words, the poetic process transports us to the universal collective myth and culture beyond our specific cultural constructs to a place, which conversely informs the individual—this can only aid in the expansion and individuation process of every human being in any culture. Once we recognize universal myths and stories, archetypes and motivations, then we can gather as individualized or individuated culturally informed human beings. Rather than feel disempowered, we become more greatly empowered through this poetic process of transcending culturally imposed limitations, finding the universal space, and then returning to culturally specific aspects and a greater understanding of the collective.

     For instance, all cultures have a story of the fire bringer as transformer of culture and stories of creation. Sharing these stories can enrich human culture rather than limit it. We understand that these stories are metaphors of human experience, and, on one level, metaphors are culturally transcendent even when they may be culture specific.

     Thus we may understand "In the Beginning: Bantu Creation Story," the creation story of the Bantu people of Kenya as one that suggests the Big Bang (*Across Cultures*, 282). In this story, Bumba walks alone in the dark in the waters, and one day the pressure is so enormous inside him that he vomits out the sun, stars, moon, earth, and then the creatures of the earth. These creatures then create more of their kind, which suggests procreation and furthering of all species. He then vomits out men and creates for them villages and instructs them of their duty to protect these wonders. Clearly the vomit is a reference to the disputed Big Bang, or a similar cosmic phenomenon that provoked the ordering of our galaxy as we know it. Clearly Bumba's message to the people to protect the wonders of the earth is a reminder that we all learn to live in accord with one another. The idea of harmony and respect for life is also coded in our ancient memory—not just the negation of it.

     We may understand, too, the Quiche-Mayan story of creation of the world through a heated discussion among the three wise men—a familiar reference no doubt to a trinity or grand council—who finally agreed on what to make happen and who, from chaos, created clarity. They said, "Let there be Light," and there was. In this manner, they created other beings and also mankind. In this story, too, they left the wonders of the earth to the care of human beings to ascertain their cooperation and conscious evolution for the preservation of life and its principles. All of this was effected by language—herein, is the power of poetry. Poetry insists upon the co-reality of something, anything, as known and experienced through the word, through consciousness. Hence, poets create worlds. Such differing worlds with similar stories of the making and unmaking of peoples are revealed in similar fashion in various cultures.

An Indian story of creation tells us of the churning of the oceans, from which arose the sun, the moon, the stars, et al. The *Devas* (gods) held one end of the rope, the *Asuras* (demons) the other end. In the churning, the pure elements become separated from the poison that the *Asuras* had poured in the milky waters (Milky Way). The only one to handle the potent poison, Shiva swallowed it and stored it in his throat–hence, its bluish color. This duality of good and evil is prevalent in all cultures, as the basis for teachings in religious texts.

Furthermore, all cultures have a story of a culture hero or culture god, one who deeply affects cultural consciousness in many ways. Stories of the fire bringer who changes cultural development forever are commonly known. The spider with the fire on its back in an East Indian story, the deer whose antlers carry sparks from constellation to constellation in a Native American story, Prometheus (foresight) who steals fire from the Greek gods of antiquity and brings it to mankind, and also the *pramantha* (churning of stick with tinder to make fire) from early India.

Such stories are passed down from generation to generation to tell us of the power of knowledge, wisdom, and, I must add, the power of poetry to affect consciousness. Several stories do, moreover, suggest changes in the skies–and, since we share the sky and the constellations, we must share stories and archetypes, hence collective memory. The old crone whose words people may fear but who is a soothsayer at the edge of town; the grandmother who tells stories and passes on tradition; the wise old man–seer, shaman, or scientist; the trickster who could be an uncle or lover; the Orphic character or the Pied Piper or a pop star who beguiles people away in a trance. The list is endless.

Further, if mythology is a recording of events in the skies, as most creation stories suggest, then we may be looking at shifts in the astrospheres. Each new era, which emerges, is dominated by particular qualities as ascribed by the constellation of dominance. For instance, the Age of Aries, which was the shortest, was the age of war and expansion. The Age of Aquarius—supposedly to begin in a few years or one that has already begun—is said to mark the age of peace and harmony. Stories of cosmic transformations abound in folk wisdom in many parts of the world. It is no wonder today that bookstores are also filled with texts on peace, change, and connecting with the heart. These themes seem to be needed in these days.

It is well known that the creative process is birthed in chaos, what to the polarity therapist is known as still point. Chaos and darkness are the universally accepted and understood archetypes with which we all grow up. All creative people experience frustration, as did Bumba; all creative people must go through a conflicting mental process like the three wise men according to the Popol Vuh before they can find the language that will clarify their creation; all creative people churn in their own psychological-mental-emotional-physical dilemmas before they can manifest with clarity and create order.

Additionally, when I ask my students to write an essay or a poem, some of them go into a state of confusion and despair. What next? Confusion is a healthy thing, an archetype or blind force of the creative process, I say to them. It's good for them—this way they can find a way out of it, suggesting that the finding a path through the confusion is exactly the desired effect of the confusion in the first place—then they have arrived at clarity and to a different meaning for themselves. We must mirror to them such ideas of positive thought. Hopefully, this develops their cognitive ability, the power of remembering, their intuition, and also their self-confidence.

I do find, moreover, that after some of these exercises, they come to feel more at ease with poetry, with their uniqueness, and with their silence.

Creativity, then, must be an universal archetype. Cultures share universal traits and characteristics–names differ.

Legends and myths are larger than life, and we are also concerned with things that are small everyday impressions and occurrences—albeit, these also contain and suggest archetypes and archetypal relationships. While at the same time, we may use symbols from our individual collective myth, we also universalize them into a shared experience in and through the poetic process. We come out of our cultures and find a depot for a shared experience—whether tribal or nuclear, we share archetypal stories of the stages of life. We also lose ourselves in order to find ourselves.

The idea thus is to get our young writers and all audience, be they readers or students, to this shared place first.

Yes, cultural critical pedagogy suggests that we help students to look into their cultural heritage in order to learn and succeed in basic college writings and classes; that we walk them through their cultural indicators so they can empower themselves in the framework of a dominant culture and within its institutions. I'd like to posit that while this pedagogy certainly has its place in some areas of academia and is very successful, a space of shared cultural concerns, of reaching for the universal and finding the particular might prove quite dynamic in the empowerment process. Yes, students need to be empowered—they need to know that, in the words of Tillie Olsen, "[they] are more than the dress on the ironing board."

They are—to continue the metaphor—the dress layered with cultural embroidery that is a shared experience. This empowerment can happen possibly more effectively through the poetic process that reveals, for it is in the revelation that people find the universal voice and image speaking to each one. Hence, this approach might be a unifying possibility because the young writers taste of their uniqueness and once they have found that, how can they lose it? I insist to them that this other place is one to which they can always return if the pressures of life take them awry. They are in awe at the richness in their inner world. This is empowerment.

In this revelatory poetic process approach, I deliberately stay away from the old academic formalist values, but instead remind the student that they must journey within, reflect on their unique experiences that are beyond cultural limitations–in this place, they find something significant and can see the relatedness inherent in all singular events and in archetypes. I'd rather ask them to go beyond culturally defined boundaries to find the common place, the common ground, and write from this perspective, instead of writing first about their specific cultural symbols.

We can return to culturally specific symbols later, once the commonality has been established. In fact, this would happen naturally.

Otherwise, I fear that in the critical cultural pedagogy, the cultural boundaries may be maintained, not overcome. I am not speaking of giving up one's culture for a global culture, but suggesting that through this poetic process one transcends one's boundaries, to find that which is universal, and then strengthen one's own cultural symbols in return–the rainbow has many strands and particles and, in its arcing above, the rainbow connects all.

For example, I suggest to my students to write about a critical creative moment in their lives, or an initiatory experience, or an event or moment that transformed their thinking or way of seeing the world. Then we find the unique commonality in each of their experiences. I have found this process also to be effective in my multicultural literature classes. However, if we ask them to write only about their cultures, then they could remain bound to those symbols and experiences that are culturally specific. Maybe, a discussion on the universality of culturally specific icons, symbols and rituals may also bring about an expansive understanding of one another.

In one of my classes, we discussed a beautiful poem titled "Nani" by Alberto Rios. The poem is about Rios' relationship with his grandmother, and it does contain images specific to his Hispanic culture, but the ideas contained are universal. We all relate to the idea that for most grandmothers, butter means love. All *nanis* love to feed us even when we cannot have more. Most grandmothers love to tell stories and many of us, if we've been lucky, have sat on their laps being so regaled. A remarkably astute point that Rios makes in his poem is very simply that even as he eats *albondigas*, he becomes aware that he has forgotten the words of his language. He is losing touch with the culture of his birth.

The two things with which we know a culture best are food and language. At its best, oral transmission and food have been, and continue to be, instrumental in connecting us to various cultures. Words and remembering words are another kind of story telling. So we talk about the specific words and flavors that accent our singular lives in our cultural framework, and we share stories about our grandmothers or grandfathers. This inevitably leads to sharing by remembering the things that matter and also then connect us with our cultural lineage and our universality.

Discussions of various related subjects inevitably emerge in the classroom. And as we continue to discuss Rios' poem, I point out the poignancy of some lines and fine details that make the experience real to all of us—not all of us are Hispanic, but the language specific details don't matter any more, for the universality in the poem allows us to know each other intimately—we are all touched by the emotive details in "Nani." Then I ask them to write a poem about their grandmothers, for most grandmothers are the same, dripping with butter love. Now, we have all become aware of the universal in each of us; thus, the culturally specific details bring an added dimension. Now I, too, can experience *albondigas* and others can appreciate *aloo parathas* and *elaichi chai* or *spring rolls* and *kimchi* or *sauerkraut* and *pfeffernuse*.

It is also interesting to discover that the word for grandmother and grandfather are same or similar in many different lands and cultures. In India, we use *nani* and *nana* for grandmother and grandfather respectively; in Italian, grandmother is *il nonno* and grandfather is *la nonno*, with an emphasis on the "n" sound. Rios' simple use of "nani" is inviting. His poem—replete with rich layered imagery—reflects a universal experience in a bi- or multi-cultural framework. It is the universality that makes the experience of knowing all the more poignant.

Nani
By Alberto Rios

Sitting at her table, she serves
the *sopa de arroz* to me
instinctively, and I watch her,
the absolute mamá, and eat words
I might have had to say more
out of embarrassment. To speak,
now-foreign words I used to speak,
too, dribble down her mouth as she serves
me a*lbóndigas*. No more
than a third are easy to me.
By the stove she does something with words
and looks at me only with her
back. I am full. I tell her
I taste the mint, and watch her speak
smiles at the stove. All my words
make her smile. Nani never serves
herself, she only watches me
with her skin, her hair. I ask for more.

I watch the mamá warming more
tortillas for me. I watch her
fingers in the flame for me.
Near her mouth, I see a wrinkle speak
of a man whose body serves
the ants like she serves me, then more words
from more wrinkles about children, words
about this and that, flowing more
easily from these other mouths. Each serves
as a tremendous string around her,
holding her together. They speak
Nani was this and that to me
and I wonder just how much of me
will die with her, what were the words
I could have been, was. Her insides speak
through a hundred wrinkles, now, more
than she can bear, steel around her,
shouting, then, What is this thing she serves?

She asks me if I want more.
I own no words to stop her.
Even before I speak, she serves.

(First published in *Whispering to Fool the Wind*, copyright Alberto Ríos, 1982. Reprinted by permission of the author.)

      Languages are sweet to the ear and to the tongue. Note also, for instance, a Sanskrit word for someone or something precious—*priya*. Meaning dear one, *priya* brings us to our oft and variously used "private"—in Czech *privat*. We develop affectionate names for loved ones and, somehow, we relate with such names even if we are not from the same language or cultural group. As a sweet corruption of "mummy," I called my grandmother, "Mimi"—the name stayed. And inspired by my exercise to my students, below is a poem in which I address my connection with my grandmother.

Mimi, Our Lonely Jasmine

Her delicate beauty like jasmine
fragrant in morning air trails along
as she collects for her prayers
hibiscus—full, red, yellow, even pink.
Red for the goddesses, white for the gods
by the altar where she and nana prayed.

The chanting sequed from one ritual
to another, the eating, the feeding
ginger drinks, guava jellies, jams —
Everything laced with butterlove
and we poking fat setting around us
complaining with laughter.
She'd freeze mangoes for us all —
children for posterity.
Before the tree was cut down,
1978 — before nana died.

Now Mimi knits silently alone —
silver-grey patterns falling over shoulders.
When she awakes at four she believes
nana's spirit roused her for prayers.

Now she waits in her quiet spaces
for our sparse visits. We are dispersed.

She'd like the children around her
mangoes breads leavening in her hands
fussing over stoves and our shoulders.
When I call her 10,000 miles away
she wants to know if I am eating well,
says I should not stay out late at night.

Now she tires more easily. Her face
has receded into bones and sorrow
has darkened her eyes as she knits—
this wilting jasmine. Ailing, dreaming,
thinking of the dead, she waits
for the arms of Mother.

Now she is a huddle of bones
stretched skin sharp eyes hollow,
she chants feebly of Mother

she knows
something that we do not.

My grandmother to whom feeding us was a religion now lies drifting away. When I visited her three years ago following her accident, I was shocked and pained to see what had become of her who chose to live alone despite suffering from a form of epilepsy. But people make choices about their life, and there is not more we can do to assist than they will allow. Now she is here and not here, reminding me that our elders often keep secrets that go with them, whether they be about family or about their own salvation. When they become physically destitute, dying becomes a long wait in a strange bed. This journey is not only theirs, but ours too–it is a painful journey for all.

Of course, our discussions cover other topics, thereby adding to our enriching experience of this multifaceted world in which we live. Note this culturally rich poem by Peter P. Ngo who, subtly and poignantly, reminds us that mothers all over the world weep for all children.

I Am a Mother
By Peter P. Ngo

I am a mother of a South Dragon
Lying on the coast of Pacific Ocean.
I allow my son to get married with a fairy
coming from the Lake of Destiny.
The couple gave birth to hundred children

With my permission, fifty sons go on the mountain
with their Dragon Father.
And the fairy mother led fifty daughter
Return to the Sacred Water.
I am a mother
of million brave soldiers
struggled against the Northern enemy
thousand years ago
to declare independence
of the Southern Land.
I am a mother – a sorrowful mother –
standing, seeing my internal enemy children
fought each others, without stopping killing their brothers
year after year, for what, I don't know
I only know I love them all
I cry when they died
I embrace their bloody body, praying
Stop the fighting
because you are of the same origin.

(First printed in *Return to Sacred Waters* 1997. Reprinted by permission of author.)

    Mr. Ngo, who has himself suffered separations and struggles during the bloody and painful Vietnam wars and incursions, has come to this place of recognition with humility and integrity. He speaks from his deepest truth, and I have admiration for his courage and simplicity. Connecting with him recently brought great joy to both of us. I was able to remind him, for he had forgotten, that I remembered him fondly as a fine poet. I recited his poems to him to make him remember.
    We know wars continue. And while men, women, and child-soldiers lose their lives, mothers all over the world feel the ache. So do fathers. So does the earth–the eternal womb so full of stories. Again his poem "I Am a Mother," so clearly speaks of not just one mother but all who give birth and see their children be killed for no reason.
    On another note, a poem that we all enjoyed in the multicultural literature class is "Yonosa House" by Appalachian writer R.T. Smith. In this he speaks of his grandmother whose music became alive in everything that she did, whether it was cooking or weaving, so much so that he hears her "chants in the thrush's song." He notes that when she died, "She sank like a root to be Georgia clay / No Baptist churchyard caught her bones." She kept her Native American spirit alive for all time.

Inspired, student-writer Heather Ratliff notes of her grandmother in her poem, "Mum," that "My Mother, my love, guided me/ as the wolf guided her," and that she "spoke the language of all those who have/wings...." she notes that her grandmother has wrinkled "perfectly." What a fine comment on the wisdom of aging—seen as a state of grace in many cultures. Stories of our forefathers also bring us together.

Oral transmission is a passionate exchange of stories. It is through stories, even moments, that people come alive as their history comes alive. What is common to all peoples all over the world are births, deaths, initiations, creative outpourings, the search for gods and chalices, the search for the self, wars and the ensuing grief and tragedy, and definitely a search for peace and transcendence. This latter is important for a new consciousness that we must today forge, so that we can keep our humanity alive within us and create environments which sustain our survival with dignity.

✦✦✦

One of the ways in which we can assert our dignity is to make our work, our presence a gift. Then poetry becomes a gift, not words collected out of a need to vent. Words arranged in poetic lines that speak of despair, of self-abnegation, of blame, of self-pity do not make poetry of transcendence–they have a place in society, of course.

However, what we want today, I imagine, is poetry that elevates the spirit, takes us out of our ordinary place to a place beyond ourselves, where we find ourselves. For we are more than our mundane-ness. Moreover, we have the power to elevate our cultures and offer them with pride. Thus by sharing ourselves, we practice becoming truly fully human.

This point of our belonging, our humanity, is driven home by student-poet Vu Dung's poem aptly titled "Every Me is Me" in which he argues that each person is connected not just in six degrees of separation, but, perhaps, just one. With utter clarity, he notes, though a friend is a friend of a sister who is married to another friend, that though someone is black or white, that "... where they come together/ they create the whole world/ Everything in this world belongs to each other."

Can it be said more simply that we are interrelated–that, in the words of Vietnamese Buddhist monk Thich Nhat Hanh, "we inter-are...." And knowing this we offer ourselves in our truth and in our beauty–transcending ourselves and our cultures and partaking of them.

Finally, in as much as we desire beauty in our lives and wish to create it, we must also then look not only to the words but also at the shape and the lines that constitute the architecture of the poem itself. For it represents the beauty of the human body and the human spirit. In the recognition of that Self ultimately is supreme beauty.

I suggest that it is our duty to create beauty—so we dance in a new way to express the new humanity as it unfolds.

I close this chapter with a story from *Still Point*.

XVIII.

Once upon a time, there was a girl-child who loved to play in the garden. One day, she stumbled over a tuft of grass. Father came out of the house, but he didn't hear her cry. So she cried louder and harder and found herself in a dense green forest standing under a tree and playing a flute.

At the sound of fluted melodies, several jungle animals came out and stood entranced. There were monkeys, gorillas, lions, tigers, elephants, giraffes, wolves, other animals and many kinds of birds. The young girl grew bigger and continued to play the flute, like Lord Krishna, the blue god who used to dance in rural splendor to the tinkling of cow bells, to the laughter of joyful women, the god who as a child stole butter and milk from many neighbors' homes, and who was the beloved of everyone in the village.

One day it began to rain very hard. Even as she played the flute, the rain came down harder. This naturally brought the peacocks out to celebrate the fertilizing of the earth after a hot dry summer. Monsoons are a beauteous time of the year. Everywhere it is green and fragrant and lyrical. Songs emerge from the air with the fragrance of the rain meeting the earth. Rainwater is the sperm that impregnates the earth, suggesting a mating of that which is above and that which is below. The girl was happy; she had found her music. In the music was her secret garden. That which is secret is sacred.

Soon after the rain stopped, boatmen came rowing up the river. They were on a mission to the villages surrounding the forest. They came with bags of dreams. They were going to slip a dream into one window of every hut so that each person in the village could have a dream, a good dream. It so happened that one child was left without one because the bag had leaked in the water, and the boatmen were short of dreams. The child felt despondent and began to cry.

Some moments later, a huge eagle flying above saw the weeping boy and dropped a piece of bread for him. The boy picked up the bread. It didn't look as interesting as a dream, but being hungry, he ate it. That bread transformed his life. It made him become alert to what was happening inside him—that was his awakening imagination, his inspiration. He learned to see with his inner eyes. He learned that the dreams were within him, and he became full and happy. Now he could go places and touch people with his dreams.

He was so happy that his body began to move in wild and happy ways. He realized that if at any time he was bothered by people or the environment and if he moved in this way, he could free himself of all unwanted influences. This movement might even be a way to walk in crowded cities. Everyone would move aside; even the traffic would make way for him. He saw himself walking through cities with a group of joyful dancers and friends and followers of that walk. He saw paths opening up to them. Opening for him.

He walked into the forest and saw there the girl playing the flute. Their eyes lit up with recognition and acceptance. Their joy made the earth wiser.

He realized that when one plays the flute and walks the dance, one can become anyone one wants to. The transformation is through the sound, through the movement, and it happens far and deep in the memory of the cell.

Thus does the dream become light; thus does it become reality.

✦❖✦

Exercises ~

1. Transmission of cultural value.
Think about a lesson you were imparted about a value. It could have been about respecting elders, about respecting your space and not making it dirty, about love or sharing, about respecting knowledge. What did it do to you, for you? How do you practice it now? Did you lose that knowledge? Are you regaining a sense of it in a new way? How do you feel about it now? Does it give you a sense of place?

2. About an elder.
Think about an elder in the community. What does he/she look like? How does this person dress, smell, speak? How does this person stand as a reflection of the cultural norms and values? What does this person teach you about yourself, your core, your history—even the history of humanity?

3. About name.
All our names have meanings. If not etymological, then there is an associative meaning. What does your name mean to you? Where does it come from? How does it sound? What does the sound convey? What vision do they see in the sounding of their name?

In my multicultural literature classes, I divide the students into three groups. They are each required to chant their name. We begin with one group, the second chimes in, then the third. One is asked to become silent, while the others continue. We establish a harmony and then gradually each group becomes silent in turn. It is quite fascinating to hear each of them chant their own name and then play this harmonics. They develop a different relationship with their name, and some have even gone on to research their genealogies.

Coming as I do from a culture where all our names have meanings of some significance, I find this exercise terrific fun and very powerful–knowing the meaning and vibration of our name reinforces our place in the world.

4. A typically ethnic neighborhood.
Write a descriptive poem about a cultural or ethnic neighborhood humanized with a narrative or epiphany of the human condition, perhaps, the spirit and beauty that sustain it. Through this experience, you may also experience your universality. And if a strangeness engulfs you, then explore that emotion—for, in that, too, there are nuances that bring you to commonality, even if as a loss. Be open to the experience.

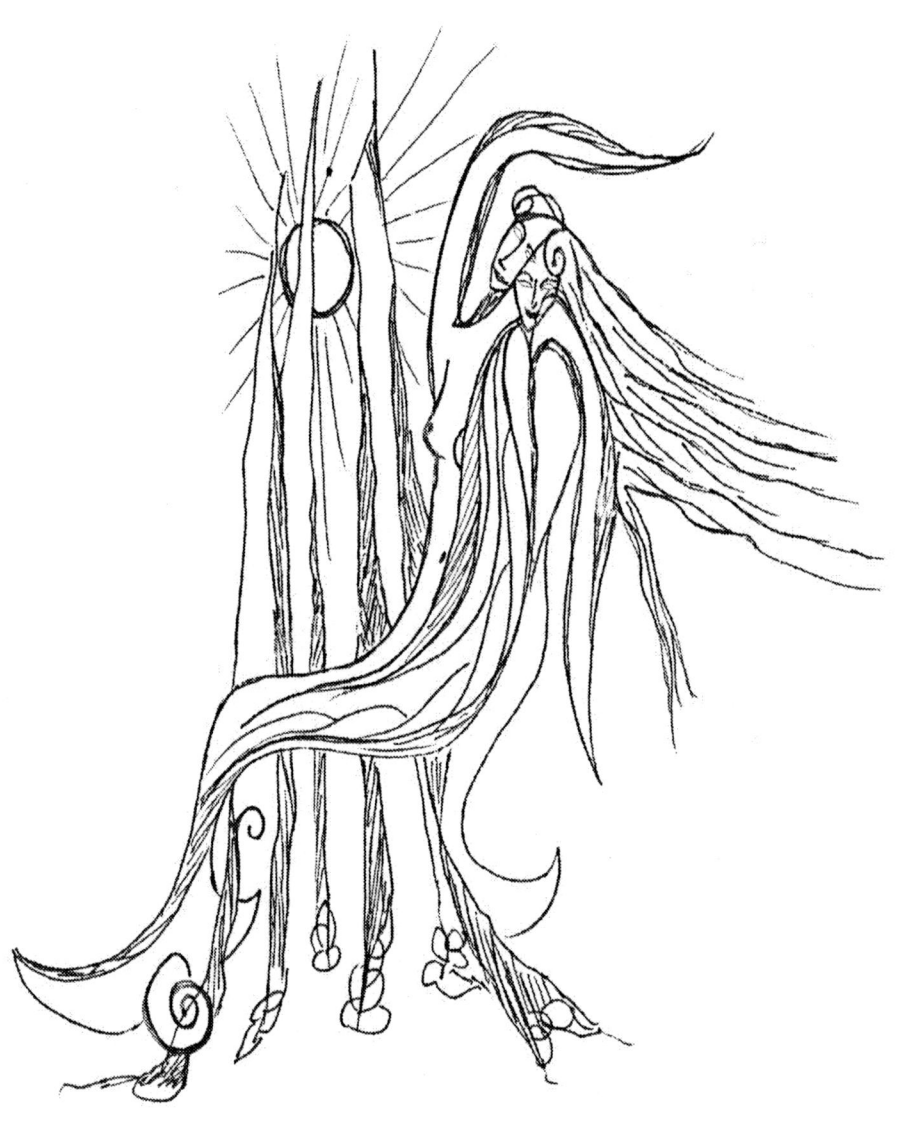

CHAPTER 4 ~ Body Architectonics

A thing of beauty is a joy forever:
Its loveliness increases; it will never
Pass into nothingness; but still will keep
A bower quiet for us, and a sleep
Full of sweet dreams, and health, and quiet breathing.
                John Keats (*Endymion*, Part 1)

    We desire beauty and wish to create it. I make this assumption because creating beauty is close to my vision and I believe that many share this. Not only our writings but also our environments must express the beauty of the inner core so that we are more aptly inspired to create more beauty. When a poem, a building, a painting, or a dance is an expression of beauty, its power is the recognition of innate universal truths–this then aids in our evolution. In our full human capacity, we are beauty.

    Romantic poet John Keats noted simply that, "A thing of beauty is a joy forever." The Transcendentalist Whitman wrote, "I sing of the body electric"; indeed, dreamers, be they scientists or artists or naturists, intuit and express a celebration of the self in its beauty and the desire for it in their works. They are knowers and when they "see" something truly wondrous, which inspires their whole being, they are experiencing that beauty, that marvel. This beauty is often times the expression of the truly simple in the that-which-is. This realization then inspires us to create forms that are poetic in our external environments.

    Certainly, we need more truly inspired poetic forms in our environments–both verbal and physical, even architectural. Our homes, schools, and public buildings must be paeans to the finest elements and the most refined in human experience. For they then move us to our betterment, unlike ugly architecture (and much of it abounds) which is a travesty to our spirits.

    So much of current architecture is lacking in elements that heighten and develop human potential. Closed, boxed in spaces; tiny windows; airless hallways; grey cement walls with neon lights–as though human beings were subjects for experiments, as though they were beings without soul. The truth is otherwise–our environments can destroy the essential human in us by taking away our ability to breathe, which is to live, to be inspired, to aspire, to dream, to know the truth, to manifest an envisioned destiny.

    Classrooms are often closed in spaces made with grey cinder box walls, lit with energy-draining fluorescent lights–the spirit cannot be fully alive and vital in such spaces. Apartment developers care less for the quality of human life than for the extra few millions that they make. City landscapes are a crowded morass of structures that look as though they were designed from the debris of a human mind. When enclosed spaces lack the poetry of movement, flow, color symphony, and grace, how can a body feel alive? Or dream alive? Or be in its vital presence? Indeed, we have a plethora of prison poems, of spirits trapped in indulgences and of violence. It's a good thing that many prison poems are imaginings of freedom, of windows of release. It is again the transcendent imagination that keeps these people alive. What if our urban environments were beautiful, would we have so many prisons?

Body architecture must be considered in the planning of living spaces in order to keep alive the harmonics of all structures. *The Wireless Anatomy of Man* by Dr. Randolph Stone is a fine illustration of body architectonics, for it suggests a perfect flow of energy and energy fields—one that is in balance with all elements. Energy lines follow specific direction and flow that compose and maintain proper patterning to keep us in harmony with the universe. But mental, emotional, physical stresses of our civilized lifestyles break this pattern and negate the human-divine principle with which we must live, forcing us thereby to work even harder to maintain our equilibrium.

Our bodies are the landscape of our souls–so much happens in here that affects our destiny. So much memory is guarded in our cells that we must consciously work on releasing the same in order to regain our innocence. I know that when I face a beautiful work of art, I am not just moved critically to appreciate it—I am, in fact, moved in my whole body. Architecturally sound buildings also have this effect on the human body. Flowing lines and well-lit spaces are a must. All elements—earth, water, fire, air—must be balanced in a finely wrought space. My entire being pulses with the power of such work, and I know then that I have come face to face with something immense, grand, marvelous. All my cells dance as they are infused with the light of the work or with the memory of beauty which re-ignites in them the sweetness they must need in order to remain perpetually in a state of health, pristine health.

Furthermore, our natural worlds provide us with much inspiration to develop spaces that incorporate light in a more beauteous way. When the body is so moved to be a powerful repository of experience, it is mandatory, I believe, that we all, especially as poets and artists, study anatomy and physiology.

When I took a class in anatomy and physiology and read of cells working in a myriad ways, absorbing and pushing things aside, engulfing and digesting bacteria and so on, I wondered at the trillion poetic happenings in our bodies in nanoseconds. That which is seemingly infinitesimal is magnified in our consciousness only when we become aware of it, which awareness transmogrifies our human experience into poetry—a constant revelation of all human possibilities within the grasp of a single human cell (self).

I began to look at images of athletes and dancers differently. These were not just bodies doing things I could not do–these were bodies in tiny specks of motion. Body architectonics in motion–words, dances, buildings moving in integrity with core.

I cannot help but repeat the notion of observing the grace of the muscle as it propels the athlete forward. The small movement of the wrist as it flicks to return the ping-pong ball. The concentration in the stance, the eyes of the golfer working on the precise spot that he would hit club to ball—the way he arcs his body. In that swing and in that arc is a poem—the body has played its music, the physiological infusions have transformed the moment, the ball is high in the air, mimicking the arc of the golfer, and it lands on the dirt either to bounce again and come to rest, or to stop in the sand like dead weight. How exquisite the expression on Maria Sharapova's face as she throws the tennis ball in the air and readies to make her serve–her impression on us all, only to win the Wimbledon in 2004.

A single motion, a single gesture, the arrest of a series of muscles in one striking pose makes a poem as does the precise arrangement of words. For in this focus is a complete universe—visceral, sensory, and illuminating. Watch the diver readying for and then taking off from the diving board. Watch the ballerina moving her arms while her pointed feet touch the earth with a delicate firmness. Watch the basketball player reaching out and over the basket to drop the ball ever so simply through the hoop.

Effortless. Mindful. So it seems. When all is in balance and in flow, life feels effortless. In complete focus, it is thus.

For years, people have taught and experimented with how best to teach poetry to high school and college athletes. This might offer a way. Reaching athletes through their strengths might produce amazing answers and poems. Let them express from the cellular level, their experience (the mitochondria action) in their muscles; the sweat, the heat, their focus and their sense of triumph—the metaphors available to them through their practices are a treasure in poetry, in consciousness. That they can find their grace in what they do and transform it into words—their physical experience transmuted into a body of words, their stories and myths would bring them to another level of understanding of themselves, making their poetry, one of pure undiluted beauty, grace, tension, and passion.

The fact of our muscles undergoing this fascinating mitochondrian function (producing energy in cells), the fact of our tendons assisting, the fact of our minds knowing clearly how the body must move in intimate relation with external factors and knowing how to navigate with all that is outside became particularly clear to me when I took a class in anatomy and physiology—it ought to be mandatory in schools. So I humbly submit that budding artists and poets take a basic lesson in the subject of their bodies. For then embodying such truths would become more real and more convincing to the writer and the reader or audience.

Abstractions embodied would be easier to grasp, inviting a wider audience. Sharing one's experience becomes simpler when one makes the transcendent experience concrete.

But first one must develop a rapport with one's own body architectonics, for we have too readily given up our power to external authority. Becoming acquainted with my body was a fascinating journey in itself for me. I came to it through holistic healing practices, and it was a challenge to make my poetry concrete.

However, it was worth it, for holistic practices and listening to my body also heightened my intuition, which helped me to trust the process in the classroom. I found that some of the polarity principles worked very well in regular English classes and I used them. These principles had to do with acknowledging the body as the recipient and vessel of information. Since the body is the receptacle and our cells hold memory of all experiences, using the principles of receptivity and resonance showed me how to significantly use this in class to recognize good writing from bad writing. I was fascinated by the results and most enthused at the wondrous openings my students expressed in class, as I urged them to open to their "knowing-ness"—also an empowering process.

Non-academic, of course. Why not! It's time for a new poetics—the old one, before poetry became an academic project. So I experimented.

Once again it was a new semester, and I was confronted with the task of meeting a new batch of students (Fall 2003). On our second meeting, I met again students' fear about reading poetry. An older gentleman said that he had not read poetry because he could never understand it. I noted that poetry is the language of the body and its rhythm is the rhythm of language, which comes from the heart. I shared with them that early poetry developed from communal chants (simple drum beats as heart beat) that ancient people performed to commemorate the elements. There were still glazed looks, and phosphorescent lights amid grey walls did not, cannot help.

Then out of the blue, I took this chance. I suggested to them to listen to their heart rate or feel or read their pulse. They complied. I felt gratified that in one meeting they had come to trust me and indulge me in my idiosyncrasies. Some felt their hearts, others their pulses. I then asked if anyone wanted to share his or her experience of it all. Am- noted that it reminded her of her sadness, noting that the sadness was because she is not always herself. I asked why. She said because things take her away from herself, what she really is and what she wants to do. I asked what makes that happen. Is it work or cultural demands, or just being too busy taking care of life situations? She said she allows external factors to invade her sense of self, so she becomes separated from herself.

I thought it best at this point to retreat. Since it was a religious moment, one of bonding together in a shared experience, which, in this case, resulted in them all connecting with a special part of themselves and each other, I suggested they free write their experience in their notebooks. They did. I strongly feel that at this moment they came in contact again with their own uniqueness, that sensibility which makes them special.

We then read Rios's poem, "Nani" (see pg. 32). I think the last exercise had already opened them to the taste of the poetic—the deep voice, the deep texture, and the deep emotion. This was not as hard for them as it might have been. And they discovered the cultural connection in the poem with their experience in a way that they hadn't ever before. Their awareness of it all had shifted. Their "eyes" were opened–so were their hearts. Naturally, I was to some "weird, man," but that is beside the point.

The amazing discovery that Jos— noted after the pulse reading was, "I feel I can write about anything." What a feeling of triumph! I felt immensely gratified that he had experienced an expansion, a kind of liberation. Ni— wrote in his journal that this was the first time he felt so real, so connected with himself. His half-page expression about his pulse reading revealed to me that he did not get this in other classes, but here. The point is that he had found a place to connect with himself, so he could easily do the same in other classes, in fact anywhere he was. He had found a clearer connection with himself, his poetry and it resides in his body, in the consciousness of his body. He had made contact. He could now move in any way he chose.

Life is layered and shaded—polarity principles remind us of opposites. So, through any conflicting ideas or connections, we might also come in touch with our shadow aspect–that, too, needs to see the light. Beauty, itself, is in the dance between opposites (harmony in discord where the discord is also transcendent like counterpoint). And the point thus is to recognize the difference. It is not without substance that our Caribbean sisters and brothers say to each other, "You are beautiful-ugly" when they want to remind someone of their beauty. This is so people don't become vain or arrogant. Good thing.

Beauty and grace of physical form is reflected not only in our bodies, but also in the arrangement of lines of poetry. The architecture of the poem also speaks to us—here I tell of the break of lines to indicate the most precise meaning to be conveyed. Language is powerful, and it must be used with care and precision so the meaning is conveyed with simplicity and grace. A poem must also look good on a page—as does the human body in its naked simplicity.

There have, of course, been experiments in concrete and language poetry for instance. Concrete poetry certainly plays with the idea of the shape of the poem matching the theme, while language poets explore the levels of meaning in linguistic play as perhaps resonating with deep cultural or individual psychoses or myths. Such explorations can lead one into psychic realms and even nonsense sound poetry. These also transport us to another place—wherein we may find ourselves.

However, my point is the exploration of beauty. It is with this in mind that I am speaking of the architecture of the body matching the architecture of the poem, wherein line breaks make the meaning more poignant and the grace of the poem lifts off the page. Once again, we can feel its resonance physically, viscerally.

It is significant that as a biological, anatomical, physiological experience of the quantum breath process (an expansion and contraction of the universe within us), poetry is an expression of pure *Eros*. By this I mean that *Eros* is the natural state of all that is. Here, too, the exploration of that ideal erotic in our bodies' consciousness might help to influence us to move towards beauty in our lives and relationships. Why not transmute our deceptions and violations for our own healing into expressions that lift us out of our pain, anger, frustration, and feelings of lack of self-worth? Why not celebrate the *Eros* in us so that we may collectively expand into a new being?

Thoughts affect us, as do sensations–may they be beautiful in sexual union as well as in the expression of a winning strike on the tennis court.

Considering the premise that our poetry resides in our body, as explored earlier, then it has to be given form in order to be re-understood and experienced in its transcendent function. This beauty of the self must be replicated in our environments–the functional must also be beautiful. We need architecture with a conscience, a poetic architecture, a conscious architecture.

We must live surrounded by a poetic embrace: visually, aurally, spatially.

Here, I share Keats' powerful ode because it clearly illustrates the beauty of the urn and speaks of its stories (our bodies and our stories) and allows for a steady solid visual impact–no experimentation with form this time. He does not experiment with language, but he does pack each line with depth and power. I chose this poem because it speaks of paradox, of permanence in transience, of beauty, and because I very simply love it.

Ode on a Grecian Urn
by John Keats

THOU still unravish'd bride of quietness,
  Thou foster-child of silence and slow time,
Sylvan historian, who canst thus express
  A flowery tale more sweetly than our rhyme:
What leaf-fring'd legend haunts about thy shape   *5*
  Of deities or mortals, or of both,
    In Tempe or the dales of Arcady?
  What men or gods are these? What maidens loth?
  What mad pursuit? What struggle to escape?
    What pipes and timbrels? What wild ecstasy?   *10*

Heard melodies are sweet, but those unheard
  Are sweeter; therefore, ye soft pipes, play on;
Not to the sensual ear, but, more endear'd,
  Pipe to the spirit ditties of no tone:
Fair youth, beneath the trees, thou canst not leave   *15*
  Thy song, nor ever can those trees be bare;
    Bold Lover, never, never canst thou kiss,
Though winning near the goal—yet, do not grieve;
  She cannot fade, though thou hast not thy bliss,
    For ever wilt thou love, and she be fair!   *20*

Ah, happy, happy boughs! that cannot shed
  Your leaves, nor ever bid the Spring adieu;
And, happy melodist, unwearied,
  For ever piping songs for ever new;
More happy love! more happy, happy love!   *25*
  For ever warm and still to be enjoy'd,
    For ever panting, and for ever young;
All breathing human passion far above,
  That leaves a heart high-sorrowful and cloy'd,
    A burning forehead, and a parching tongue.   *30*
Who are these coming to the sacrifice?

To what green altar, O mysterious priest,
Lead'st thou that heifer lowing at the skies,
  And all her silken flanks with garlands drest?
What little town by river or sea shore,   35
  Or mountain-built with peaceful citadel,
    Is emptied of this folk, this pious morn?
And, little town, thy streets for evermore
  Will silent be; and not a soul to tell
    Why thou art desolate, can e'er return.   40

O Attic shape! Fair attitude! with brede
  Of marble men and maidens overwrought,
With forest branches and the trodden weed;
  Thou, silent form, dost tease us out of thought
As doth eternity: Cold Pastoral!   45
  When old age shall this generation waste,
    Thou shalt remain, in midst of other woe
Than ours, a friend to man, to whom thou say'st,
  "Beauty is truth, truth beauty,"—that is all
    Ye know on earth, and all ye need to know.   50

(http://www.bartleby.com/101/625.html)

    Here, I am also impelled to make reference to Samuel Taylor Coleridge's "Kubla Khan" which explores that idyllic place of balance and beauty. A poem of visionary power, Kubla Khan makes good the promise of divinity manifest in man and the mythical landscape which man can create, one that expresses humanity's manifest power, idealism and the perfect place of balance and of pleasure.

    Indeed, the Romantics expressed well that in the power of the imagination rests our enormous potential–and to create that ideal meant to go to another world from where to extrapolate the unique and the beautiful, to recreate it in the physical plane. Perfect process–let it not remain clandestine, but may it be manifest for all to experience and enjoy: this beauty in and around us that we are here to bring forth in our physical world.

◆❖◆

Exercises ~

1. Visit different environments.

I suggest a visit to different places (specially if they are new to you) and write about the physical and emotional responses to the different environments. How do these places make you feel? What details are evocative and of what? Where are you transported? What is your fantasy of the most beautiful neighborhood, home, room? How should your schools look? Would you like more parks in cities?

2. Body Architectonics.

To play with this, assume different postures and write about muscle interaction or response or emotions in those postures. This is to see how you might respond to your body in various positions–both comfortable and awkward and difficult. This is to understand better your own body and its architecture. How do we feel in different places? Do some smells start pain in a body part? Or joy? Or sorrow? What are your thoughts on the subject of your body? Do you want to know how to release them and heal yourself? Discover the universe or landscape of your body—it has infinite intelligence. Come to a place of neutrality and explore your self. Write body poems.

3. Fantasy about Ideal Place.

Imagine yourself in idealized vistas–describe those places. How do you feel, what thoughts come to mind when you envision such spaces? What would you create? Why? What is most sacred to you?

4. Fantasy of the most ideal love.

Create in your fantasy your ideal love. Experience its beauty, grace, and passion in the cellular consciousness of the body. How does this feel? How can a difficult relationship change with this consciousness? Write a poem of transformation.

5. Knowing fear.

Fear has its place in our lives and can be a fine motivation; however, it often gets a bad rap. Instead of knowing and dealing with it, we negate ourselves and others, and compound our fears even more. This adds pain to our bodies. Feel your fear, know it, breathe it, and discover your strengths and wisdom. Accept fully yourself and others, be tender. Let there be space in your body for joy.

Chapter 5 ~ Power of Silence

Poetry is an orphan of silence. The words never quite equal the experience behind them.
   ~ ***Charles Simic***

Poetry of the dancer or the athlete is sheer poetry in motion and in stillness, for poetry is also about silence. That silence is also in the very gaze that sees the movement. That silence is in the very arcing that is movement that follows/creates the movement of the ball that the golfer hits with precision. See that ball winging in the skies and you hear the silence. Watch light filtering through green leaves and you see the light in its silence.

In that silence, time expands and stops. In that silence, when you feel your pulse, you hear the silent sound of your self, you find it and you are comforted by it. This comfort allows you to expand and know, to rest and restore. This silence is also the measure between notes from beat to beat; from a single glance to object of admiration it is silence.

The most poignantly sung piece by Madre de Deus' singer is titled "Silencio"—this one naturally comes to mind. But, of course, you have to listen to it to know what I mean. You have to have your own experience of it. As her voice rises in its cogent passion, you hear it sculpting space and making form, and you hear the silence accompanying it. Madre de Deus is a small band in Portugal made famous by inclusion in the Wim Wenders' film *Lisbon Story*. The CD is aptly titled *O Espirito du Silencio*.

Here is my poem from my collection titled *In the Folds of Your Sari—Poems for Amma*.

xxiii.

If there's time for time
there's time for poetry
Time for poetry
   is time for manna
Manna is food of the gods,
   so it's time to feast.

On words

and the silences
   between them

and the silences
   which contain them
and silences which subsume
the passage of time

reflections on a shy leaf
   yellow in flowing waters
the glisten of light
   on wings of butterflies
the sweet intensity in
   your *kohl* dark eyes
the fragrance of white
   jasmine on a hot night
the taste of water
   on a dry thirsty tongue
the sounds of breathing

for Silence
devours time

Silence
is companion to Stillness

Silence
is
beyond time
an expansion
an awareness

a collective inhalation
and exhalation

and in Silence
is our evolution

truly, yes, silence
is
your language

(Also published in *VIA: The Quarterly Journal of Vision in Action*. Vol. 1, No. 1, 2003)

     Perhaps, the process of finding the poetic impulse is basically finding one's silence–the space within space, or in the words of medieval Indian poet, Kabir who defines god as "the breath inside the breath."
     Furthermore, consider how we use language to express certain

states of being. I can say that I am "moved beyond measure". So moved that one cannot measure it. But I shall play here with this. If measure is notation of space in music, then it must mean that my consciousness has gone into that other place where it will only respond to that notation, the voice or frequency of silence. If this is so, then I might add that it is here that miracles happen because one is illumined. And being illumined, one is restored. Being moved beyond measure then is being moved to the space within space of silence where one is restored. This space of silence, as stated by Yasuhiko Genku Kimura in his lecture on "Cosmic Consciousness" at Agape Church (Culver City, Spring 2004), and in many of his writings, is the place in the depth of one's being, and in the depth of the Cosmos, where "the sheer openness of Being ceaselessly opens" and "the radiant void in the heart of Being voids itself to reveal the fullness of Being, which is Wholeness as the Matrix of Meaning." So, you renew and restore your wholeness by returning to the heart of your being, the place of cosmic silence that is at once the very heart of Being itself.

Curiously, I had just such an experience of being in the "heart of Being" in the summer of 2005. I was at a camp. One activity had us working in groups, practicing aikido moves. It was my turn to be blindfolded and in the center of a circle of 35-40 people. Two big guys playing the attackers would grasp my hand and I was to move them out and over. Suddenly, out there, in the middle of the circle, I came to a powerful stillness. Everyone cheering me seemed to be eons away from me and their sounds were but muted echoes. The two guys landing in my space seemed to have leaped here from far far away spaces. And when they grabbed my wrist, it felt like a light touch–subtle and wiry. For a moment I was caught in the power and beauty of this vast immense silence and space. Then I had to act. For those voices kept coming–at that moment, I chose to not be swayed by the sounds. Here, where I was, was perfect. Is.

Later, when I recalled the experience, I realized I had come into the Tao–where is immense vast space and it is still; where is neither dark nor light and it is not darkness; where is no measured or measuring of time and space, for it is just expansion; where is just this breath that is not breath. I was so impowered (sic) by this felt experience–it was not a vision, for all of me was transported into this place–I realized we move even beyond transcendence. Silence, this beyond-transcendence silence, is the language of god.

Having been "here," I know one can go here, be here any time. And bring back the space of the dynamic stillness of this dance– for in the moment of just going there, many worlds collide, movements happen, self dances, self speaks; most importantly, self expands to incorporate all galaxies and beyond. And then, one experiences something that is beyond comparison–a feeling of utter stillness and exhilaration. It is an unknowing and a knowing. That, itself, is poetry.

Then I returned to the dance of life–none of these words feel the same now–wondering why we move from shore to shore searching for this space, caught in our dance of vanity. How can we become this space in us and around us? For, life happens and we deal with its inequities and vagaries. Would it be perhaps, by knowing our silence and spaces within that space?

This is the journey that I like to take my students on. Hence the canyon exercise as explained in Chapter One of this essay. Despite their resistance, they did it. I know from their sometimes-perplexed looks that they are journeying to this place with me. I am grateful. Even if they are not quite sure of what is happening to them, in, and around them; when they take the plunge, they return sweeter and more vitally alive, for they have shed something too.

This chapter is short–I wish to leave you with pages of silence.

The uncarved block, unmarked pages, composer John Cage's bold composition simply titled ' 4'33" '—a piece of music in three parts containing not a single note—just silence, and people paid to listen, to be attentive, and they laughed heartily. Something must have shifted. Cage believed that there is no silence, that in the silence you hear a variety of tones or ruffles. Perhaps, silence is a state of awareness—or that it is a state that brings one to a heightened awareness.

This silence—the breath of dawn before the sun clips into our waking moments, the moments slipping into a heightened aware dream state. This silence—the gap between our heartbeats.

◆❖◆

Exercises ~

1. Sitting in private space.
Sit in a private space, turn off all noises one by one, shut all doors, and then focus within to the sound of your heartbeat. If thoughts come and go, it is okay. Ultimately, you will hear the silence. Then you can more easily find your stillness. Even if it is but for a few moments, it is good. Write about how it feels and what you know of your silence.

2. Sitting in a crowded noisy café.
Here, focus inwards to seek your own stillness. This would help you to focus on your work when you need to. This experience must be anchored in your body with a singular word or resonance that is particular to you. Even if another person resonates to the same word, your experience of it is different and singular to you and you own it.

3. Experience silence in nature.
This experience could enable you to listen to the sound of the breeze, of leaves turning, birds' wings soaring. This must make you hear your own silence and you will find that you are, indeed, space—vast awnings of space within. This would lead to a poem in which you are transported outside to a world, which also exists within. Rich. Additionally, being in nature is so rejuvenating.

4. Experience the silence in a place of worship.
This must be experienced in isolation so that you can feel the divinity within yourself–not just in sermons that are external. Such a revelation might empower you to be more fully yourself. Indeed, to be awed by oneself is a powerful and humbling experience. Could this move you to accept others' similar or different religious experiences as divine? Write your experience of such a revelation.

Chapter 6 ~ The Word: The Law

The ultimate authority of the Rig Veda is said to lie with the gods, for they are the origin of thought and poetry.... The hymns were handed down from their origins in the distant past from bard to bard until they were finally set down in writing as a collection somewhere around 900 BCE.
   ~ Stephen Naylor

When we speak from that "dream state" we often speak from our knowing, from our silence–from a direct participation with our god.

This deep within Voice reconnects us with our inner impulse of speech, *Vac* or *Vak*. (Vak is also goddess of speech—utterance.) In Sanskrit, *vakya* means sentence, *vaad vivaad* means debate, *vachan* is promise, *samvaad* is a collective discussion. A thought once spoken (given breath) held weight. In ancient times, speech was revered highly. Words were not to be used lightly. Anything spoken was taken seriously. Unnecessary chatter was frowned upon. After all, the gift of speech came from the goddess herself. How could something from this source be misused?

Since all life came from a divine source (and to divine is to know), life was seen to have a mystical dimension. "The people fancy they hate poetry, and they are all poets and mystics," noted R. W. Emerson, suggesting that all people are knowers. Knowledge of essence resides within.

Keeping this mind, in ancient times, the power of the word was not taken lightly. Our words had and have meaning and power. I may also posit then that grammar of language is contained in our cells–therefore, would it not be accurate to suggest that we are all poets, and we are here to create, speak, and walk our truth? Eighteenth century English writer, Samuel Johnson suggested that, "Poetry is the art of uniting pleasure with truth"–possibly that which resides in us. Perhaps, one might then question if it isn't, thus, more pleasurable to be in harmony with the grammar of our consciousness? By grammar, I do not mean punctuations or form necessarily–but a pattern of thinking that leads to clarity—is clarity itself. Critical thinking at its best! Poetry?

Indeed, is it not said, "in the beginning was the word"? And in the Quiche Mayan story of creation (others as well), it is the word, the description that brings to light all of life. Surely, then, language mirrors to us the sacredness of all life. If infusing *adham* (clay) with breath brought him-her to life, made him an a-live human, then giving him-her the power of speech was the next step in aiding him-her in realizing the purpose of life–*to create life and to live it.*

Through language, the human defined this world, this identity and the various relationships in the world, in the cosmos. Through language, he-she developed the power of constructs, of logic, of grammar–that power to express. And that which is expressed with clarity, that which speaks of truth—universal and cosmic—is surely an expression of that which is poetry and the poetic–the self.

It is the mythos that arranges in his-her mind the connection with time and space. It is the logos that establishes and explains the structure of thought and of narrative, and illustrates the intricate relationship with and within space—the matrix. It is the ethos which partakes and which, through continual participation with the mythos, creates and recreates the world in which we live. Logos serves to provide the structure.

This, in essence, is the process of coming to be and passing on. The form and the impulse of the continual emergence of the cosmos as we know it. This is our poetry—and this poetry is so eloquently explored in ancient texts.

For example, the ancient-most Japanese mythological text, *Kojiki*, contains the following sentence: "In the beginningless beginning of Heaven and Earth, the nameless Names of the Gods that make the primordial Sound out of the Silence into the Supernal Sphere of Space and Time are *Amenominakanushi-no-kami* (the God that is the Lord who is the Primordial Source and the Central Fulcrum of the Cosmos), then *Takamusubi-no-kami* (the God of the Male Creative Principle) and *Kamimusubi-no-kami* (the God of the Female Creative Principle)." (Translation by Yasuhiko Genku Kimura.) The Japanese word "*naru*" used in the text to signify "to make the primordial Sound out of the Silence" also means "to bring into existence" or "to become." Here we see a beautiful blending of mythos, ethos, and logos.

In their simplicity, early verses and utterances such as the one above express the *rta*, the law of the universe, the dance. In their depth, they illustrate ways by which human beings can maintain harmony in their lives, in their perpetual relating with their universes. This poetry expresses the beauty of nature, the skies, the animals, indeed all of life with terrific eloquence. Since the universe is structured and in harmony, one part in perfect relation with the other, and each singular element is measured in its place, so, too, must poetry emerge in perfect meter. It does–breath brings rhythm in language. Breath and meter produce the inherent harmonics in the poetic consciousness.

Further, poetry in bringing one to recognition serves also

a kathartic process that brings us to a new consciousness again and again—making it, thereby, a revelatory experience. Revelatory because it reminds us of our relatedness with all the elements: it is about space and measure, it is about time and motion, it is about stillness, wherein we experience our movement and forms come to life–both in light and in darkness, for the shadow is also in stillness and present to guide us.

Indeed, everyone is a poet. For each person creates his or her own universe in a constant interplay with the forces of the universe–internal, external, and eternal. This is a process of coming to our truth, which then affects all of humanity. Has it not been said time and time again that, in the words of Percy Bysshe Shelley, "Poets are the unacknowledged legislators of the world"? Are not then poets the creators of the world and of destiny? Participants in our evolution? Aspiring towards and integrating with their own divinity?

According to Irish lore, the Milesians arrived on Irish turf, were not welcomed, so Amergin, a Milesian, offered to leave. When he and his men were leaving, the De Danaan, people of the goddess Dana, used their holy men to raise up a storm, which Amergin calmed with his own druidic powers. Three days later, they defeated the De Danaans and established dominion over Ireland, wherein he promised Eiru to name the land after her. His inspiring and universal song offers a glimpse into the powers of poets–to claim to be and know the inner workings of all elements and living beings and, thereby, to claim dominion over all.

The Song of Amergin

I am the wind that blows across the sea;
I am the wave of the deep;
I am the roar of the ocean;
I am the stag of seven battles;
I am the hawk on the cliff;
I am a ray of sunlight;
I am the greenest of plants;
I am a wild boar;
I am a salmon in the river;
I am a lake on the plain;
I am the word of knowledge;
I am the point of a spear;
I am the lure beyond the ends of the earth;
I can shift my shape like a god.

(http://www.angelfire.com/de2/newconcepts/wicca/amergin.html)

Being creators, poets are thus godlike. They make and change people, cultures, and nations becoming then culture heroes. Note the effect of musicians and public speakers in and on our various cultures. They succeed because they touch our core, despite our various and polarized experiences. Unfortunately, some influence despite their lack of connection with light and integrity.

When people go through the polarities of experience and find their truth that they are committed to walking with the destiny that they create–the dance that they compose, the conclusions that bring them to their center, with or without struggle. Truly in that search for balance and our singular truth, we often walk a fine line.

A former student, Joseph H. Cho (formerly Hyung Cho) composed a sonnet in perfect iambic pentameter about his meeting with his truth–it is a poem of victory.

A Sonnet on Perseverance
By Joseph H. Cho

When looking back upon my life I see
That moment where I should have fled but stayed;
Despite the cautions of the pow'rs that be,
As yet my conscience I had ne'er betrayed.
To cut one's losses and begin anew
Would be by far the wiser choice to make;
But as the busy worker bee is true,
I swore: "My firm resolve no fate shall take!"
Bring forth the torrents and the stormy winds;
Subject me to the worst you have in store.
When tempests die and shadow dark rescinds,
Alone I'll stand like heroes of great lore.
It matters not that I succeed or fail,
As long as what I hold as truths prevail.

(First printed in *Saltwater Taffy* in 2004. Reprinted by permission of author.)

A remarkable young man whose writing was always precise and a wonder to read, Mr. Cho shows us that a heroism sometimes comes with a sobriety and sombre resolve that invites us to review our own passages and decisions. Then we also acknowledge the teachings of our darkest moments of indecision, despair and thorny indulgences— as he does, nay, he calls upon challenges through which he is resolved to remain with his truths.

Peruse a poem by Kathleen Duncan–a sestina about her journey for truth. A sestina is not an easy form to emulate—but one that can be rewarding.

A Silent Scream
By Kathleen Duncan

The world I once thought
was fixed in all that is truth.
I believed that clarity was eternal,
that is until I had fallen,
deeper and deeper, in an endless crescendo.
Where is the light?

I wandered, grasping, seeking the light.
Bombarded, no, tortured by my thoughts,
pushing, driving, into that terrifying crescendo.
When it diminished, there was still no truth,
and I realized how deep I had fallen.
Into darkness, darkness that seems eternal.

I imagine that only this, nothing more, is eternal,
that life is only a slowly fading light.
I perceive that it Is not I alone who has fallen.
I can no longer see the value of thought
as I weep, mourning for truth,
but I hear only that deafening crescendo.

Mankind, an orchestra, enters that horrible crescendo–
it never ebbs, never diminishes, but screams eternal.
And in all the deceptively harmonic mess, no one hears truth.
No one bothers to uncover the light.
We all turn away absorbed in thought.
So absorbed, we can't see that we have fallen.

Into doubt and despair we have fallen.
Unable to stop or even to slow that awful crescendo.
We have been deceived into believing that thought
will lead us to all that is eternal.
All that we see is ourselves, in a distorted light,
as we claim that what we are seeking is truth.

How can we find it, when truth
Seems, along with all of virtue, to have fallen?
When we cannot even see a flicker of light?

We seem to keep tumbling in that endless crescendo?
Why bother if nothing, if no one, is eternal—
And we are driven away by our own thoughts?

We must first see that not all thought reveals truth,
and that which is eternal has never fallen,
but leads us through that awesome crescendo, into the light.

(First printed in *Saltwater Taffy* in 2004. Reprinted by permission of author.)

    The note of completion in the poem sounds like a welcome bell. It reminds me that the responsibility earned in finding one's truth is that then one is compelled to walk it as well. So the poetry continues to unfold with its singular polarities taking us from dark to light and back and forth. This poem above is powerful in its intensity and in its truthfulness.

    The poet arrives at her point of light. This revelation is spontaneous, even as the language lends her its own unfolding. The spontaneous revelation happens without our knowing it—it is a surprise that hits us, connecting our individual consciousness with the greater collective in a fusion that carries one beyond the physical plane—and this physical plane is not a contradiction, but a grounded continuity. We are brought down to earth at the same time and made humble, not just by remembering our own experiences, but by following the poet's own expression of her truth.

    What Ms. Duncan arrives at is her authentic voice and resonance. There are ways of finding resonance with little moments in our life. One is by finding words of resonance for ourselves that match the feeling of an experience. The word may change as we also do. For each of us, there is a singular specific word that keeps us in synch with our core or wholeness. If we navigate our cells with open aware neutrality, we can surely find that word, and we can then anchor it in our bodies for ready retrieval. So I was ready for another exercise in the classroom, albeit on a small scale–to recognize good writing from bad, to be reacquainted with the grammar inherent within of the harmonics of language.

    Once again in the classroom, my heart beat nervously as I looked at the students and asked them if they wanted to try a way to recognize good writing from bad writing. I was also excited at the anticipation. They intoned, "yes." So, I began my explanation. Interestingly, this was a class in composition, and writing a coherent essay is a challenge to many of them. I told them that grammar of language is coded in the body–that if they paid attention to what constitutes good writing, they could program themselves to recognize and fix their writing.

So we started by reading a really badly written paragraph, replete with errors both mechanical and grammatical. I asked them to register the sensation in the body–they were able to pick up the negative resonance and identify it in the body. Sometimes, I help them with this process by feeling in my body a particular student's sensation and identifying it for them. Then we read a beautifully written paragraph– they could feel and know the difference. They also received this one in their body–the grand receptor.

Terrific! I then asked them to find a word that matched the badly written paragraph and a word for the well-written paragraph. They received and lodged both in their bodies. They tested themselves by reading the paragraphs again. I then told them that they could easily pick on the resonance of either one and so refine their own writing by using their bodies as a reference or receiving station.

After all, if a piece of music is off key, it hurts the body—though localized in the ears, the entire body experiences it. Mozart has a very different effect on the body from, for instance, acid rock or grunge rock. Naturally, if we respond pleasantly to finely stringed music arranged in a pleasing harmonics, why not an essay?

I have used this principle in other writing classes in order to reveal to the students that the power of language in its precision and beauty resides in them and that they have already in them the skills to recognize good writing from bad. I urge them to use this experience to their advantage. My wish is to empower them with new skills and with the tools inherent in them—their knowing of their truth.

It is for all of these reasons that I wish to expose my students to the space, stillness, and sound within them. Hence my assignment that they go to the canyon at the crack of dawn in their solitude and experience the quiet splendor of the sun clipping over the horizon. I want them to listen to the breathing of flowers awakening, to the sound of the dewdrops, to the birds on low hung branches orchestrating their new day.

If we as educators and poets can bring this consciousness to young poets, what a transformation we might effect. If we as educators and poets can reach out with our truth and guide people to their truth, what impact could we have on our evolution—how we think, act, believe, behave, how we are in relatedness with all that is sacred, or secret, is then affected. It cannot be otherwise.

Poets of yore have recorded such experiences, have known of the power of the word in its perfection—like a "globed fruit"—and I may here assert that such a consciousness cannot, does not, will not allow human isolation. When we have all tasted of this place, it has to affect how we become and how we relate to everything that we hold significant–*life!* Then we cannot be in our separateness—but be whole even in separation.

Let's call all our selves together with the one word that brings our resonance to the core—and it is a different word for each individual person. Let that word be your poem—a single secret source of remembering and re-collecting, gathering and being whole.

It is a moment of completion from our otherwise disparate selves. We, as holistic integrated conscious selves, are the promise, too, of the poetic process.

♦❖♦

Exercises ~

1. Game of interactions.
The aim of this game is to take you out of your comfort zone, forcing you as a co-participant to break patterns and find your resonance. Shifts will occur in the process as you relearn what "feels" right and what does not.
a) You are blindfolded and walk with a partner around the room. You may be asked difficult questions while you navigate your way in this space. Questions may be about your sense of self or your habits. Stuff may come up–be aware of what happens and what emerges. If this makes you think of how you do not wish to be, then make a note of it.
b) In the blindfolded state, you may be handed a variety of objects to touch, taste, or smell. Note your reactions to these. What do these make you feel? What comes up? What memories? Note them and your reactions. Can you find your center through this exercise? Can you find your new word or expression of resonance?

Once you have identified the old and the new spaces, write action steps to take to show you how to achieve the new or different level of awareness. Certainly note down your new word of resonance and relatedness. This could lead to a new poem—tap into your creative self.

This could also be a weekly exercise and journal to help you to be in touch with your inner knowing.

2. About harmony and integrity.
Write what these words mean? How can and will you remain in integrity with your core? What does it mean to be in integrity and in harmony? What takes you out of it? How do you return to your integral core so that you keep your universe in balance? Remember that we need emotional, psychological and structural integrity to remain in health. What is your language of wholeness?

3. When the shadow speaks.
Shadows and demons are powerful teachers—they may appear in dreams or be aspects of people you know. Explore a fear or a shadow image or figure. Be intimate with it, for it reveals a teaching for you and your universe. Remember dark chaos—when everything seems to break down in and around you? What is the nugget you find?

4. Make up your own.

Chapter 7 ~ Prayer of Gratitude

At times our own light goes out and is rekindled by a spark from another person. Each of us has cause to think with deep gratitude of those who have lighted the flame within us.
 ~ Albert Schweitzer

It is significant in our lives that we practice being in gratitude.

To express my gratitude to my readers and my students, I must make an utterance. I must praise you and experience the wonder of our interaction. I must invoke the highest good and the deepest space within you to receive me and within me to receive you. Hence, I must speak the right words. When I am in resonance with my deepest truth, I cannot but speak the right words. One way to ground such utterance is through the power of, what I call, creative gratitude. Then we may walk with our truth more fully, more simply.

Creative gratitude is a process of coming to this place of being in gratitude through the poetry of thankfulness, through the creative process. This may be sourced, in an experiential workshop, from the physical and emotional body, again using the principles of polarity and resonance. Of course, one can come to this place of one's own volition.

Perhaps, thankfulness may be one of the hardest states of mind to achieve in our lives. After all, for some odd reason, many of us suffer a shyness that prevents us from speaking our gratitude. Perhaps, our hearts are closed and we fear reaching into those spaces of relating, for we feel vulnerable. Perhaps, we fear what we might say or receive. Perhaps, we feel we deserve more. Perhaps, we become arrogant and expect the world to serve us for being here.

But then something happens and we can lose everything–sometimes, this dispossession can lead us to recant and transform; sometimes, it can lead us to greater disaster. We choose. And if we choose the becoming in goodness, we remember to be grateful for all the difficult situations that may have robbed us of our equanimity, our health, our self-esteem, our entire sense of self. But then when we have found ourselves–this is a poetic experience–then we can move forward in different ways of expression and cleansing.

So we cry tears of gratitude. We cry tears of mercy. We wash ourselves as we restructure our bodies, our lives, our thinking.

As grammar pays obeisance to its structure, to its self, so, too, is the impulse in sentient beings to express gratitude for this order. The ancients knew the power of thanks—it was a way to maintain humility for the grandeur of the universe, reminding us that we are indeed cosmic dust. Here, to be reminded that our main purpose is to respect at all times the harmonious order of that which is—the cosmos, the cosmic forces, indeed all of nature, ourselves.

Thus, our relatedness gives rise to many forms of expression—dance, art, poetry, all of which are expressions of the self to celebrate everything that contains and feeds us. If so, then these expressions transport us in our consciousness to a more complete reality of that object and in our relatedness, we re-relate, we return edified. We also make our offering, our contribution to the world, because it is our duty to do so. It is our act of gratitude.

This gratitude is a prayer—a prayer is simply a way to remember to be grateful. It must not be a form of subjugation or of control, but of relating with a simplicity that reminds us all of our existence with each other. This also reminds us of our tears—what are tears but god's kisses?

Thus, an attitude of gratitude transfigures us so we find our pulsing wholeness in our beatitude. We are then become transfigured into our poetry. If we create from this place, we create beauty.

This is the poetic relationship.

Thank you. For you, I am grateful. Here is a prose-poem letter on gratitude.

Dear Precious One ~

I keep forgetting to think of you, to write to you–get busy with everyone else–so sorry. Even as I say this…this so sorry, it tastes just a little bit like betrayal.

Guilt like grit delivers itself in my mind for all the sorrows I caused you–never intended, never malicious. Just for forgetting you–I am truly sorry. Just for losing you time and time again–won't happen again, unless…thank you for still being…

I want to thank you for reminding me just yesterday of who I am and what I mean to you. And then I remembered. More…

Thank you for the hurt, the pain, the separations–dark lessons, which that made me long more for the light. And longing, having tasted of it.

Thank you for the prisons, those walls around my heart, the silences that would not come apart. They found me many voices–colors and words and opening doors of my imagination.
The sages tell me that we make doors open–we also make them shut. It's our thoughts that count. That make matter move.

Thank you for the blocks and confusions–bruises and contusions—good lessons in the art of mind-expansion, to rearrange me in harmonious order, to protect me from my ignorance.

Thank you for the grace of friends and mentors for showing me the light. For the meanness of petty moments for showing me golden shields. The power of the word to slice the heart–the power of a glance to open it. The power of the smile to connect all the clouds.

I wrote one day, I wish my heart would grow so big that if someone stabbed it in a part of it, I would not feel it…I still do…

I love watching birds against the sun clipping skies–the waves that make me run in them, their foam making me laugh, as my clothes become drenched.

Like soaking in the liquid love of grace that courses through my body–when I know I am home in the many arms of sweetness. I play at being more greatly mindful of such moments of resonance.

Thank you for showing me how to play–drop the worries to the dust. Those worries that bring not grace but dust of forgetting in the mouth.

Thank you for my senses that allow ancient voices whose beauty is coded in my DNA consciousness. And for the ability to recall our golden moments that sing in luminescence in all our cells. And for the tones of poets from all times whose voice is the *sutra*-keeps us connected.

Thank you for the lessons of the darkness–that surge once in a while to remind us of strengths to know the light. To smile.

Thank you for this journey—the bends in the road, the spikes in the mountains, the bitter winds, the dust that finds places to settle.

For the path of the swan–splintering the sky turning in many blues, of golden hues and pearly evenings–many thanks.

Many thanks—and when my thanks become a collective sculpture that can come to rest in the stillness that is poetry, then I know your will is done.
When I look at you and see your eyes beginning to mist over, I know I have come home.

And I must forgive myself for being lost to myself over the years.

Let me pour my thanks and forgiveness into one big bowl—silver and golden
Let me slip in a bejeweled copper ladle

Let me be of service—you mean so much
Let me hold you in my palms like the universe
Let me stroke your hair and arms
Let me hold your feet in my lap
Let me taste of the bitter fruit of truth—the light of understanding
Let me be my child again…

Thank you – for you.

    I close this chapter with words of John F. Kennedy–"As we express our gratitude, we must never forget that the highest appreciation is not to utter words, but to live by them."
    As we become gratitude, we become love.

Exercises ~

1. What are you grateful for?

Make a list of everything for which you are grateful, even the smallest thing you may not think about, e.g. the grass under your feet. Look around you and see the things you take for granted but which serve you in some ways. Feel gratitude in you. Write what this new relationship does for you. How does it change your life?

2. For whom are you grateful? To whom?

When you feel sad or blue or pathetic, think of other people. Remember why you are grateful for their presence in your life. What did you learn from them that makes you who you are? We learn from so many people, from books, from chance encounters, from someone walking by that opened something in us. Take a moment to remember them and write about them. Separately, of course. They can be very beautiful vignettes of expression of your prayer in the world.

3. Transform your self-perception.

Regard yourself carefully in a mirror. Thank yourself for everything you have accomplished, loved, shared, given, received, learned, struggled with and for, challenges you have overcome, tragedies you have mourned. Write a poem to praise the simplicity and grace you are seeking within. This, too, is empowering. Remember not to put others down while you boost yourself, for doing so would weaken your own growth and transformation and your poem.

Chapter 8 ~ Being the Beloved

Love came and it made me empty
Love came and it filled me with the Beloved.
    It became the blood in my body,
    It became my arms and my legs.
    It became everything!
Now all I have is a name,
    the rest belongs to the Beloved.
    ~ Jalal-ud-din Rumi

The universe is a matrix of the interplay of *Eros*–the stuff that holds it together, the stuff it pulses with, and the stuff with which it perpetuates itself. *Eros*—a self-creating thought from which all else emerges or emanates. *Eros* is love–an action, process, attitude, and condition that moves our universes.

What then is better than to write about love? Love as that elusive force that hides and lies low. Love as that blinding light. Love as that which rouses itself in us and moves us to find another of like resonance. It is this that must make unions happen, not mere custom. Love, itself, is customary.

Everything we do, I share with my students, is an act of love. For it is that which motivates us. Now this may be a confounding thought, since there is also much violence in our world. Just lack of that love principle which, prompted by fear, creates barriers and walls and devastation. No one is free of love or fear–no matter the social status or role of leadership. Not you, nor I. The conflicts and difficult situations with people close to us or far from us, the violence in cities, the wars from times past to now all indicate the hapless fear of crossing boundaries and finding a place of balance–that equanimity which is also love.

Yes, wars have been fought for love as well. Does this mean then that warring is not about loving? Or that the dialectic of the universe, the conflict, is a part of this strange interacting matrix of *Eros*? The sad part is that we get caught up in anger, fear, betrayal, deceptions, and hurt. What then? Our ancient stories are replete with such stories. For instance, Paris falls in love with Helen and we have the Trojan War. In the *Mahabharata*, the Indian epic, the five brothers, the Pandavas lose their kingdom over a game of dice to the 100 Kauravas, and almost also their wife, Draupadi, who is saved by Lord Krishna, guide to the Pandavas. Later, the *Mahabharata* war occurs for the Pandavas to win back the home kingdom—this epic includes the message from the *Gita*, a revelation through Lord Krishna's sermon on the cost of not taking action and the cost of taking action. In this case, taking action is as much an act of love, as in other situations when non-action may be the act of love. Perhaps, what we have to look at is what is there to win or to lose, and what the act of loving entails–for loving is a condition of the living principle of our consciousness in this our infallible universe.

Loving and choosing to love are not always easy. Old paradigms must be cleansed so the new can take their place and re-form us. As we move out and away from old haunts, shadows travel with us. We again cleanse ourselves and move on and may be confronted from time to time with those shadows and the churning begins again. If the stories of creation arising from the churning and resultant purification of universe matter are true, then our correct thinking at such times of similar churning in our personal lives brings us out again from the shadows into the light of love. We are infused again with our own radiance–love moving in and through us, keeping us synchronous with the all-encompassing *Eros*.

Such a process can also illumine to us our beloved–both within and without. And realizing this is a most beauteous expression of the self in its completeness, polarities intertwined, the yin-yang in motion, Shiva-Shakti in balance perpetuating the universe through erotic play.

So, we move in polarities—in a spiraling formation, individually and collectively, and we learn what love really is. This is part of our evolving to a clearer and more expansive definition, feeling, and acceptance of love. But first we must re-learn what love and loving really mean and feel. There are many ways by which one can come to such an understanding.

Spiritual teachers, intent on spreading the message of love and loving, have a hypnotic impact on the audience. We desire such messages–we want to hear how important it is to love one another not only because there is so much violence around us, but also because we feel separate, isolated, alone. However, many of us grow up not knowing what love and loving really feel like, so conditioned are we with expectations, definitions and limitations imposed on all our expressions. Even muscle testing attests to this state. For we discover through other kinesiological processes that even emotions are learned expressions of human intent and action. Love is also one of them.

Yes, we feel moments of love, we feel caring, we feel anger, we feel loss, and we feel grief. We are taught we must love, be honest, be generous, et al. Yet, most human problems and ailments stem from not really knowing how to love unconditionally. For the love that we learn is conditioned by parents, cultures, institutions, who are conditioned by their predecessors. Perhaps, some change is required in order so that we perpetuate communities of people who know and understand real loving–so we practice in order to learn and know the elegant art of negotiations for balance and harmony. It is not easy, but necessary.

One way to do this is by reprogramming ourselves to know what love feels and looks like through the practice of resonance techniques as earlier explained–by calling on one's inner most place of knowing to flood all cells with the memory and light of love and anchor it in the body.

Another is by working with the core belief/Orian technique as taught by Vianna Stibal. One of Vianna's teachings is to reprogram us with the information and knowledge of what love truly is. This is done by accessing and communicating directly with our various levels of being and perception. With her techniques, we learn that we can release completely the negating beliefs and thought patterns that prevent love and loving and bring in that which we all desire–we can become finely attuned to bringing in the magic of love and remind us of what love really is. Once we relearn this love, we are better equipped to grow in confidence and radiate our truth. Such processes, of course, are poetic. They happen in the inner core of our knowing, which knowing occurs on many levels of our being–physical, mental, spiritual, intellectual, auric. Once transformed we continually affect the universal matrix.

But what does this have to do with writing poetry?

Mystics know well that all knowing comes from a profound quiet place and may be expressed in various ways—through color, through sound, through words, through deeds, through thought. Commitment itself to the loving is the passion we need in order to make any waves in the world that are worthy of our existence on this beautiful planet. Commitment to this love gives us the power to love another completely and fully, whereby surrender, too, becomes a passionate fulfillment. Yes, all of this sounds easier written here than practiced. Writing it feels good—the process, itself, is a challenge on many levels.

What does it mean to surrender, to love? For one cannot surrender what one does not know. Thus, it is necessary to know what surrender and love truly mean and who we truly are. Only then can we truly surrender ourselves to the loving, as it reveals our inherent mystical nature. And then we may be transformed and recognize better that all universe, indeed, is *Eros*. How lovely to pulse with it and be transformed! Not easy, but certainly heroic!

Recall Peter Ngo's poem about the nectarine on page 17. How elegantly Mr. Ngo shows us his beloved transmuted in the universe of a nectarine. Here also is Aurelio Gerard who writes in "To My Dearest Love" that a fiery and freeing loving brings him more than happiness— he writes, "that in finding love I have found a light / And beauty around in all I see." He notes that prior to this love, he felt lost, and now he promises to love completely. Clearly, in this his impassioned love, he also displays aspects of loving the precious beloved, for he wishes so much to protect her and the love itself.

Inviting the beloved then is a supreme act and sacrifice–when the beloved is nigh and within, we become love. We become that which we most desire and cherish. Look at the ecstasy of one who truly knows the divine, not one who is taught what the divine is–for the latter, it is not a lived experience as it is for the former. For our own edification and fulfillment, we might prefer to know love and the beloved in direct communion. We must directly experience love and also the divine in loving–for then we become what we know.

This experience may also be true in everyday mundane relationships–then they are not so mundane any more. Institutions acting as conduits to explain the divine to us take away our power to know. We must know it here in our bodies, so we resonate.

So how shall we learn this process of being fully ourselves? How shall we merge this consciousness in our new world? By expressing that which we are. By being true to our deepest silent core. By holding the space for the beloved. By then becoming the beloved. By being in complete integrity with ourselves–for then we "canst not then be false to any man." as Hamlet notes in Shakespeare's play (Act 1, Sc. iii, line 80). This is a coming to recognize who we truly are in our authenticity. It happens in waves.

My experience with such a process of recognition has not been easy. The polarities have their sway. We wander from conflict to conflict as we encounter challenges, particularly those in the area of relationships. Of course, we attract one of like resonance–but it may not match what we have created in our minds. In order to do that, we must then raise our own consciousness and bring in the greater resonant being. Sometimes, it may be through trials and sorrows—as we evolve, we become clearer, for we are also in a cleansing process of what has been stuck in us by parents and cultures.

Additionally, I've been told that such a transcendent beloved may show up for an instant or stay for a lifetime. However ecstatic or painful it might be, for this one time it was for an instant–this connection that had happened for several life times and came like a clear direct knowing, came but for a few hours. When you know from your core, you are not wrong. You just know. I had such an insight, and there was a quality of recognition, but it was not in the right resonance. There was but a deep cellular communication and that was it. After that, vast distance. When this happens, one has to let the person go–it is best for both persons involved.

It did not help that I had written a poem about such a moment two months before the brief incident. It did not help that I had explored the beloved in poems some years ago. Perhaps, it was prophetic. But our body knows the smell and taste of sorrow and of love. Our body does not lie–we must train ourselves to listen and to receive. Our minds can lie to us–our lower minds, not our transcendent minds.

The poem "Transparencies" was written in response to a phrase in my poet friend Sarah Luczaj's e-mail letter to me. She had finished her letter to me with the sentence, "My husband says the day is strangely transparent." That line felt so alive and vital that a poem poured through me as I responded to the note. I had a sinking notion as I wrote this poem that I would have to experience just this–I did. Good thing, I had a poem to mark the occasion for myself. It brought me to a willing chuckle–the *aha*! of knowing that I knew it all along. Words and phrases reveal–they take us to that place of knowing and bring something forth. In this case, this poem.

Transparencies

Love's luminescence
whose eyes are strangely transparent
but know how to hide, shy away...

And I want to see more
but hold back (turn away)
for rippling the waters
of that which is so private
that you don't see it (or won't)
And I just might.
What then?

Shall the layers of seas crinkle
and crack like egg shells
Shall the sky fall on our heads
Shall we curl up in our toes
and hide our smiles

Or shall we stand like trees
those Ancient Ones
who know so much
for roots that go through worlds
What then shall Love do?
In luminescence, transparent.

Such strange words are these
Such strange lips that speak them

And eyes that see
and seeing not —
they hide behind fine gauze
of shying woven eye lashes

Seeing your eyes in mine

And the green, oh the green
resting with lavender
Sunshine in the moonlight

a broken cup
spilling wine
love's rivers...
        indecisions?

      This next poem also came like a light from above–this time from the shower. One day in about 2001, feeling sad I started to weep in the shower. As I felt the water on my face, I suddenly had a thought that the water falling from the shower were the tears of the beloved washing the tears of the beloved, mine. I was transformed, excited, thrilled. The moment was redefined since I had been transported to another place which was mine and where I found myself. I wrote then the following poem.

Who is the Beloved?

What is the beloved? you ask.
The beloved is someone whose feet
you kiss as you bid goodnight.
What is the beloved? you ask.
The beloved is one
in whose eyes you see raindrops
drifting on falling leaves.
What is the beloved? you ask.
The beloved is someone whom
you can smell with your touch.
What is the beloved? you ask.
Someone in whose belly
you rest your aching head
and whose being you cradle
in your whispering arms.
What is the beloved? you ask.
Someone whose words shatter

your stillness and carry you
to greater self-knowing
whose ears wait to hear
the resonance in your voice.

What is the beloved? you ask.
Someone to whom you feed
the food of desire from your mouth.
Someone to whom you feed
the food of rest from your hips.
Someone whose thirst you
satisfy with dewdrops
shining on rose petals.

And when it all comes down
to moments
when the world is a shattered mirror,
the beloved is just that someone
whose tears you wash with your own.

Who is that beloved? you muse.
It is I, I say. It is I.

(Previously appeared in *Words for Hungry Tongues*, Inevitable Press, Laguna Beach, © 2000)

    The beloved is all this and more when all boundaries dissolve and there is no separation—you cannot tell sugar from its sweetness, or water from its wetness, or the sky from its expansiveness. Sometimes, when the beloved is expressed in the dynamics of the body, the poem can also be disembodied, for the emotions and play in the cells follows the logic of the grammar of that *Eros*, when all senses are in happy disarray. That does not mean that the poem is ungrammatical–just that it is real and makes complete sense as the experience is transmuted in words. Most of all, it recreates the world for us, renewing it and bringing us to transformation.
    The following poem—not disembodied—was written as an experienced idealization of that embodiment of sweet resonance.

7.

My limbs are become the conduit
of your passions, your dreams, your desires
and your breathing — I partake
of your pleasure, and of you
from your eyes —

Do I see with mine?
Or with yours?

It's lovely to see the world through
another pair of eyes – what an elliptical orbit
what a dance what new rainbows what tears
what cracking skins of hands that have known
many worlds and much toil and dust

It's lovely to see the world through
another skin and to breathe it all in

It's lovely to be your conduit
in receiving you – I become more me —
More more more me…

Breathe into me – breathe through me
I am your breath…
savor me.

There mountains gullies ravines
Ochre emerald rusts and the cool of autumn…

Here my supple skin my tongues —
savor the space between us
the liquid of us…

all worlds are same…

    Perhaps, love is a process of understanding that, essentially, all our worlds are the same. Or, perhaps, it is poetry that brings us to this place of understanding. Whichever the case, arriving to this understanding is a long negotiation once we have tasted of it in our imagined experience.

    Moreover, it is true that poetry brings to form and to reality moments and interactions in our lives, defining reality and relationships as we unfold. In this context, we can see poetry also as a way of activism, for poets have reorganized the world, nay even created it. Such acts of recreating must come from the motivation to explore truth and beauty and then be conditioned by it—for words and language define our reality and our evolution. Choosing to co-evolve and co-create are acts of deep love or, perhaps, of conscious love.

    If everything we do is an act of love, then writing poetry, too, is an expression of love, not only for ourselves but also for our community. In fact, it is our duty to do whatever we can to bring more love into the world through whatever channel or action we wish to take.

For, is it not true that, eventually, it is our very presence that becomes the embodiment of that to which we aspire–to be the Beloved!

Then we meet with our beloved.

❖

Exercises ~

1. Playtime.
The beloved loves play. Look into the mirror in your quiet time. Enjoy yourself; luxuriate in the magnificence that you are. Write about the beloved in you. Write many times. There are so many faces of you. Love yourself. Write about what it feels like to be the Beloved. You are the mirror of what you desire.

2. Envision the Beloved.
Write a description of what the beloved feels, looks, smells and sounds like. Metamorphose the experience into a transcendent place and write your beloved from that quiet place. Tears make this place rich in a unique and cleansing way. So does laughter. Sometimes it might also help to check in with your pulse beat. Who is this beloved you desire? How can you become this beloved, so you find it?

3. Eye-to-Eye Contact.
In Chapter 2, I discussed an exercise of looking into another's eyes and being open to what appears. This may be repeated with a focus on receiving the divine imaging and embrace. When you feel that you can surrender to such a loving presence, then you know that you are in contact with your beloved. Write what you experience. As Ralph Blum notes in his description of the Sowelu Rune, "Even in loving, it is Love that loves through us" (Blum, 132)

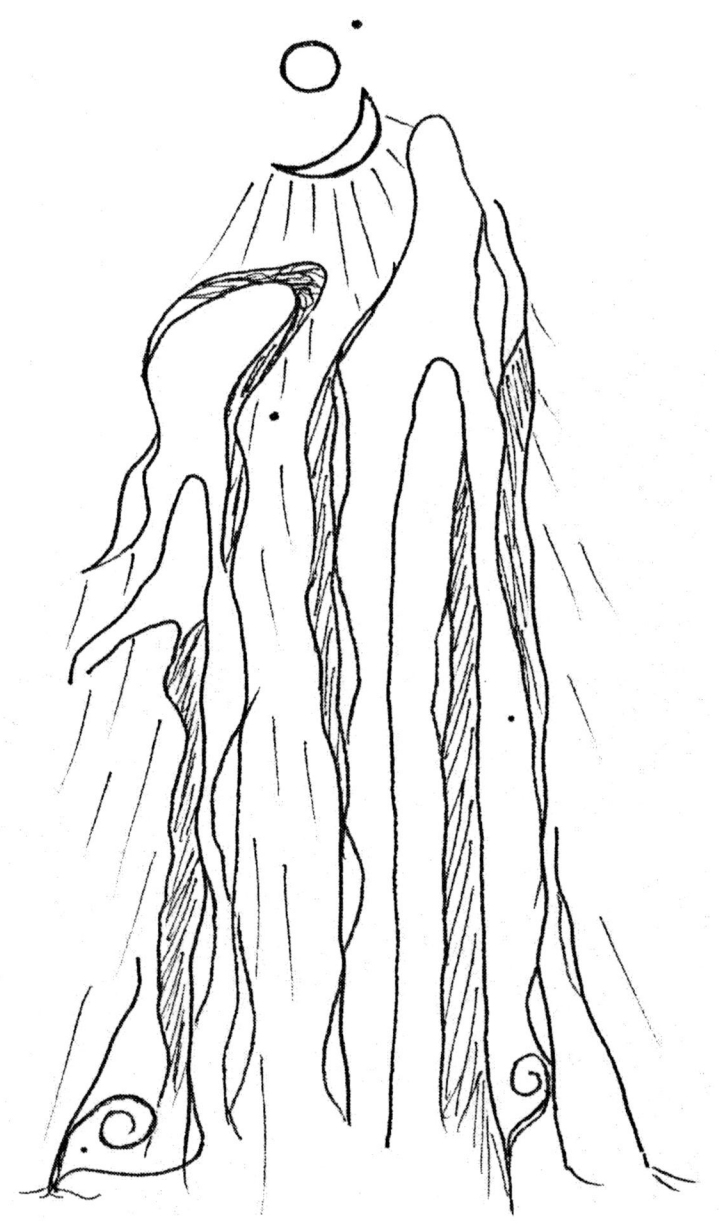

Chapter 9 ~ Poetry of Source Within

Ethics, too, are nothing but reverence for life. This is what gives me the fundamental principle of morality, namely, that good consists in maintaining, promoting, and enhancing life, and that destroying, injuring, and limiting life are evil.
  ~ Albert Schweitzer, Civilization and Ethics, 1949

"The Sanskrit root matr-, to measure, is the source of the word for matter itself, as well as material, matrix, metre and maya - the Indian concept of the illusion of measuring and dividing that we live by, and from which we must eventually free ourselves." http://fusionanomaly.net/sanskrit.html

In the beginning was thought. Self-existing, self-creating, self-directing thought.

In the expansive-expanding golden matrix of our consciousness, we are self-sustaining, self-evolving and self-restricting. We make, move, or mar our very own at all times. Why? There seems to be a gap in our knowing and in our willing and in our doing. Why? There is this terrible duality in our subconscious to which we succumb despite our many warnings and our many lovings and teachings. Why? There is this negating principle in our midst. Why?

All this takes place despite the fact that we do know better. For haven't we been told stories and given teachings, been lectured at and punished? For some reason, man has believed in his own supernal power for which he thinks he does not have to give thanks. But he is wrong. He has to give thanks, and he has to do that which is right.

The only way to do this is to connect with this poetic principle and consciousness–when we are in this place of awareness, we remember our inherent goodness. I am moved to include here John Buchan's words: "God gave us poetry out of His great compassion, not so our age can chatter to itself, but so that all ages may converse."

The ancient African tale of the Bantu people reminds us of Bubba who created the world and all its creatures. He gave them each a purpose to live and also the power of self-creation. Through this process, he also imbued man with the lesson and power of compassion. He expressly said that man must take care of the beauty and wonders in the world—they were (and are) in man's care. This story was and is a revelation, but man lost the essence; however, the threads of the cord lie hidden and surface from time to time. I perceive their appearance as poetic utterance.

The story of the *Bhagavad-Gita* is essentially a message that we must do our duty. It calls us to know that we create the world and destroy it by our negligence. Once we are in this negligent mode and wreak havoc on humankind, we have lost our connectedness to all life-enhancing principles. It is at this point that we must call it back into our conscious acting selves and take action to make dramatic transformation happen. It cannot be otherwise. The time is now–to shift our consciousness in a poetic moment, in a poetic way.

Very simply, when we have discovered the "breath inside the breath," in the words of Kabir, and have recreated our environments based on the transcendent principles of love and joy, then we are in our aware meditative state—in the moment, in the now, fully alive.

When we co-create from this perspective, we are in touch with the language, the grammar of origins, which offers us the paradigm for our process, for life, simply because it is about our spiraling cycles, about our co-evolution. For as discussed earlier, grammar resides in our bodies–which, to borrow Dr. Randolph Stone's phrase, is the wireless anatomy–in whorls and spirals, that also contain the golden proportions. But this book is not about the golden proportions as much as about how poetry moves in us.

In so co-creating with our inner language, we become in touch with our core and recall our beginnings. Early poetry as is recorded was about our beginnings, which has given rise to the great mythic traditions of the world. The forming and dissolution of elements and the cosmos, as is beautifully expressed in the Shiva principle as well–life as continually pulsing motion, the constant cycle of being and non-being, the recognition of all this as contained in silence—a language of love, a force that moves the universe. Such paradigms are universal, not specific to a singular culture.

Of course, to understand the dynamic interplay of cause and effect, or motion and stillness, language must be most precise. Thus, precision may be seen as synonymous with simplicity. Simplicity with directness. Directness with honesty. Honesty with recognition. Recognition with revelation. Revelation with knowing. Knowing with silence. Silence with stillness. And in the stillness is the consciousness of movement within. So, the polarities continue; the cycle continues.

When we have come to this place once, we have recognition of it and then we can return. When we have returned here again and again, it becomes a really good habit, cleansing and revealing, connecting us with an ever-renewing consciousness–a silent recognition before the voice speaks up sending its vibrations out to the world. "In the beginning was the word, and the word was made flesh...." I see this simply as the power of the original thought to imbue humankind with its truth, and the knowledge that we are transmissions of energy with the power to direct it in accordance with universal laws. Knowledge of these laws resides in our cells, govering the conception of life and how it flourishes.

Such awareness of life force manifest in loving transformations (love also as dynamic process of struggle) cannot keep us in the dross malaise of existence. So in summation, let's look at this paradigm.

* Poetry is the power of energy given voice–a reflection of the alive and living dynamic principle.
* This living dynamic principle is a movement towards health, balance, light. If all life is contraction and expansion, wherein the contraction is manifesting of dis-ease, then this outward movement is the expansion. A moving away, a clearing, a revealing that the core is indeed light which was being crowded by too much crud–greed, deception, violence, betrayal, wars, destruction.
* The movement towards a different poetics is to highlight the beauty inherent in our matrix. For in the light, we "canst not thus be false to any man." Poetry, then, must lift us and transform us to our healing and our ethicality, a love for all life, a movement towards positive growth.
* A movement in positive growth is a path to our truth, for we know we are the Self and that all life is sacred and interconnected. Thus, we live guided by ethical principles of abundance and sharing.
* The poetic vision must guide us into our future, for poets are activists. Note P.B. Shelley's oft-quoted words about poets being "… legislators of the world." We are actively responsible in this unfolding drama of co-creation–to be driven by conscience and compassion; to share our light and gifts; to practice discernment; to attend to laws of the universe that protect and balance life. Writing is thus a transcendent act.

Certainly when we are in this poetic consciousness, this contained universe wherein we know—and this "knowingness" is that point of stillness and continuity—so in that knowing, we are connected like universal gods, we become inherently ethical. This totality of being—mind, body, spirit, auras and more—brings us to a coherence with our universe; thus, we cannot do harm to any "other" for there is no "other"—only the perpetually dancing, separating, re-connecting selves.

Moreover, this, too, demands an even greater element of spontaneous self-restraint. The knowing when the connection is desired and desirable and when it is not. And if we can become thus, we then are with our manna. The food of the gods! Our foods! Could we want more than this?

Recently, I asked someone I met to tell me something about himself. My question was, "What is your poetry?" I realized that it sounded rather odd, and I must have sounded peculiar in a way. So I wondered what I meant by that statement. Then it came to me that what I meant by that was simply, "What is it that matters to you? Who are you? What makes you?" The answer may take longer reflection—some laughter, some embarrassment, some quizzical raising of eyebrows, some irritation. The answer behind the answer, once all the stories are re-told and surrendered, may be simpler. Hmmm...

For after all what is poetry but a journey in self-recovery through self-reflection—the most self-reflexive art that is revelation?

Poetry takes us to our inherent godhood: *That moving sculpture is god—a repository-container of all frequencies (known and unknown, measured and immeasurable) in a harmonized dynamic whole dancing in its perfect stillness—Self-reflexive and inter-active-being—Sexing the universe at will and at pleasure—in truth and gratitude—blissed in playfulness–Spawning universes at will–marking infinitudes–in-resonant balance of breath and being—knowing both the dark and the light.*

Eating the Light

XXXIV.

A word, a mirror
sings of mysteries, of light

A child, I look into the water
see wild clouds
like horses' tails streaming
for the farthest apple
a fabric that wraps divinity

Water slowly trickles then drips
I extend my hand and collect the drops
and exult in its taste.

♦❖♦

Exercises ~

1. Your description of the ideal.

Explore your image of this god space, different from what institutions have taught you. What is the image and perception of the divine spirit? Transpose this into your being; feel this inside you. Do you find this aspect in all living beings–animate and inanimate? I see it in you, in the leaves, in a sliver of light that falls on the window, in a rock, in a ladybug, et al. Write about your discovery of your new self–that is a part of all that exists. Know that you are a co-creator of all life process and unfolding. That ideal divinity is you and in you. It is how you create your universe.

2. A poem about nothingness.

What is your experience of nothing? What is it? This vast awning of possibilities. What will you make of it? Write a poem of what can emerge from this nothingness by your informed, creative thinking– the *Ginungagap*, as Scandinavian myth would say. The *Ginungagap* is the space from which life emerges, man and woman are born, and the world as we know it comes into being. What will you bring into being from your experience of this nothingness? Write it down. What is your vision and gift for yourself and for humanity?

Chapter 10 ~ The Gift

A human being is part of the whole, called by us 'Universe'; a part limited in time and space. He experiences himself, his thoughts and feelings as something separated from the rest — a kind of optical delusion of his consciousness....

Our task must be to free ourselves from this prison by widening our circle of compassion to embrace all living creatures and the whole nature in its beauty.

— Albert Einstein, Quantum Reality, Beyond the New Physics

Our presence is a gift. We are a complete, complex, composite poem, and our lives are a work of art. Knowing this brings us to our dignity, grace, and our majesty.

A professor of mine impressed on me several years ago true poetry must be a gift. That struck a chord in me and I have tried to maintain such clarity in my verses. I have at moments failed, but then found that poems that even border on complaining lose their poetic appeal, which must be to clarify and universalize the human dimension and quality, to elevate the pathos as both creators and receivers of a lived, universal, poetic experience and expression.

Thus my experience tells me that poetry must transcend the ordinary in order to make the ordinary extraordinary; the poet must not remain self-absorbed in a "me" perspective, but seek and discover the "me" or "I" in all in order to discover the greater "I".

The poet must rise above his/her experience so that he/she does not leave the readers or listeners floundering in their limitations, but invite them to a self greater than their limitations in order to have a transcendent experience of the same ordinary event. We all have them—why not change the experience of them? —Or the experience of the effect of them; why not rise above and offer each other "gift poetry" instead of "need poetry"? Perhaps, this way we can change our outlook, our consciousness, for we have the ability to choose.

We can choose our resonance and we can choose to resonate with the full expression of our uniqueness, our gift.

Once again I was not disappointed. Student-poet Aurelio Gerard C. Angeles noted in his poem "I Made You" that he watched on television an ad seeking donations for people struck by poverty and hunger. He stopped peeling an orange and sat wondering about how a "loving and caring god" would allow such an abomination. He wrote that he fell into a silence and then heard a voice, "I did do something about them;/ I made you." In his "The Awakening," Angeles notes how each singular aspect of nature awakes into joyfulness at each new day. That makes him, the poet, note. "My senses opened / To the dawn of a new day / 'Good Morning!' I said." I believe he opened to his relatedness with the world, his gift.

The truly poetic then must be a gift (cultural and human), not something done out of sheer need to vent. However, rage, pure rage, also has its transformative power, but when we remain caught in anger, blame, self-negation, or despair, then we lose opportunities that the universe brings us asking us to transform. The transcendent shows us a way out of this miasma to an attitude of love–our mission here on earth.

Space here is for you to explore your own revelations, ramblings, and compositions. Unfold your *lila*. Play on—!

◆❖◆

Exercises ~

1. What is your gift to humanity?

Brainstorm how you and your life will transform the world. Transform this metaphor/image of a unique and wondrous universe into a poem.

There may be many poems here–for we have many gifts to offer. Explore the idea of integrity and what it means to you. Do you create from your integrity? How does this value shape your never-ending gifts to the world? How do you remain whole?

2. You are the gift.

Explore how you are a gift to humanity. How is your life a gift to the universe? Write your poem of your magnificence. Write many poems of your unique majesty with which you walk in this world.

3. Make up your own.

4. Make up your own.

Part II

Continuum: A Love Story

Ever wondered why institutions hang the most uninteresting innocuous installations in the name of art? Why that four-piece beige, white, and beige-grey-white flecked rectangular thing is plastered on the wall? It says nothing to me...but wait! The scratched cream floor with grey and beige tiles scattered in uniform patterns and motions. And wait! The square segments of Swiss cheese layers for a ceiling with obnoxious neon lights. Ah yes, the white walls and fawn colored walls. Not to mention the uncomfortable grey chairs fastened to the floor with steel bases and screws. It is so riveting. Everything innocuous, alarming in its vacuity. Cold! Like sci fi offices, hospitals, places where the sight of blood spills fear into the heart.

These are classrooms. Spaces where people are supposed to absorb information, but here neon lights emit that constant buzzing. This saps energy. The reason for institutions. Control.

Ahead 100 years, from where I come, we study in earthy rooms, with windows that welcome in breezes and green colors, life and movement, scents of grass and flowers. Not here. This smells of diffuse stale white light, not divine white light. This smells of oppressiveness. And the spirit does not like that.

I enter my office. The ceiling is that torrid cheese look surface cut into square and rectangular sections. I have covered the glaring neon lights in my section of the office with newspaper. Shawls or fabric would be better. The glare was always too much for me, a child of wood and green spaces. Even my friend, Isabel had noted that, yes, neon lights are dangerous. So she had left her high-paying corporate job, sold her house, and gone off in search of wooded purity, noting that even the corporate managers and workers were tired all the time. No wonder. Institutions see to it that people shouldn't have the energy to seek the natural world, that everyone is pacified into order. What they don't realize is that this order is only a patina. The chaos never emerges into patterns of harmony, which is divine order. This is what the keepers of wisdom know. They have known it for a very long time.

How do people here keep their humanity alive? Fettered sensibility. I can taste the aridity that hits me with such vengeance that I am overpowered into negation. I think that I cease to exist. I open the file cabinet, which is placed diagonally coming out of the corner of two walls painted a bright orange. Is this where my past lies? In corners? In file cabinets? Papers? Education and so much paperwork where truth is lost in bureaucratic grade making.

What shall I tell them—the keepers of wisdom—when I return

to my home with them that schools have become factories, that societies are fragmented selves pulled into a chaos of their own making, that many of those seeking an education don't have an inkling of why they are there? What did I do here 100 years ago before the world turned unto itself—inside out? Did I do any good? I am plagued with questions and reminded of my frustrations. Was I always missing the mark? I know I tried very hard, maybe my ways were different and that was difficult for all the others, whose ways were more like each other's. Some compensation that is. Now after all these years.

I've been sent back to find out where I had left my past, where it hid, where it crouched, why it hadn't traveled with me. Sometimes, it's better that way, but I needed a clue to one problem and that lay in the past. In this place where I used to work and where I am returned to find the clue, and I feel now its dangers to living organisms.

I used to become depressed and overwhelmed, feeling that I would never get up out of this paperwork and streams of memos that sap energy. I wanted to keep my energy for those that really needed it—those that came here to seek, to know. They believed that knowledge would set them free. Yes, but they were taught to enter systems that took away the divine spark. How could they be free? Or better still the question—what must they be free of? And next. Why? Why should people be free? Aren't we?

All these questions were pertinent here, in this world. Back home, we had gone past such ideas of freedom; they were too limiting. When we grow and our consciousness expands because there is space for growth, when such growth is natural to the core of every living being, there is no limitation. The self is too expansive to limit itself or the other. And it must be expansion to which we aspire.

I am brought back by loud laughter from both ends of the hall. People keep their humanity alive somehow. Courageous. A sudden loud knock on my door makes me startle.

"Excuse me, er, Professor...may I come in?" Njeri peered from behind the door. I looked up from the pile of papers in which I was buried. After hour office hours. Yes, she could come in, but I wondered what question or concern I had left unfulfilled. Grades. It must be about grades. Njeri stepped in her arms clasping her bag. "Hi, Njeri," I motioned she could sit on the chair by the desk. "What's up?"

"Well, I just wanted to talk to you about the question for the essay on struggle. I don't really know how to begin it," said this soft-spoken young woman with wide eyes. Her naturally full mouth curved despondently. I felt her frustration, realizing that the essay question was perhaps the prompt for the story of her life. And that was too overwhelming to sort out. Our lives are indeed so wrought with questions to which there seem to be no easy answers that daily existence itself becomes a Sisyphean task.

"Njeri, what do you think are the struggles of ordinary people—you and me?" I asked.

"Well, just making it,...I don't know. Sometimes I think people don't know how to get along. Sometimes I think they just aren't happy with what they have. And then, well... it's so difficult out there to make a living. And then there's all this violence, and no peace...and..oh I don't know," she said.

"Seems like you do know quite a lot about it and have a lot to say," I said.

"Well, I still don't know what to write. I mean, where do I begin? You know... this question...it's good, but...," Njeri was clearly getting very involved in the subject.

"You know, you might begin with a personal experience perhaps and objectify it from that point on to discussing the concerns of humanity that you then see as paramount today. Hmm?" I waited for her response, trying to be helpful, but feeling helpless myself at this moment.

Njeri looked thoughtfully at her hands, her brows puckered. She seemed to be getting very upset. "You don't understand," she said, "it's not so simple as you make it out to be. You know... shit!"

I sat up thinking she's right—all I know is my experience and what I want for them. Njeri continued, "I can't just do it. I have a little kid to look after, my mother's dying of cancer. My boyfriend took off three months ago and then I have these classes. This class. It's hard. How can I do all of this and I want to do well. My father...well.. he's another story...I don't want to talk about him, Ms. Manu. I mean how...?"

By now I was feeling more grounded and equally concerned. Did I bring up all this? The essay question? Images and voices alternating between two dimensions. Memories of Rene, another precious being, crowded out of existence. Found dead in her car from toxic fumes. Alcoholic family. Incest. Memories of others, all lovely souls trying to find ways to success and getting lost in the maudlin competition of the consumer world in which they lived—not long enough to know how to get out of it all, just knowing they had to, without knowing where to go. Every other place seemed an utopia, except that there was no road to one.

And here was Njeri. I felt I had to give her something, or say something so that she'd walk out of here with some hope rather than emptiness. Teaching wasn't what it used to be. A process of imparting skills, information and challenging value systems. It had become a parenting, healing, therapeutic relationship without the desired result.

I couldn't just tell her she was smart and she'd figure a way out. That sounded lame. She knew she was smart. I couldn't just tell her to let the questions ride and she'd know what to do, which, of course, she would. At this moment she needed something else. Perhaps just a space to be without judgment, without limits, so that she could hear herself say what she needed to. Clearly, she was feeling lonely.

"Njeri, it feels very difficult to be in the middle of all this. I do know that you are a powerful woman. At this point what do you need from me?"

She glanced at me as if to say I was putting her on again. "Why me? I just want a simple life…to be left alone …and live the way I am supposed to?"

But that was the whole question. How are we supposed to live and to be? Must we accept every limitation? I realized too that she mirrored a feeling that had plagued me for a while—my longing for the ordinary life. Not this one—a mythic creation of other people. One of conflict and seeming lack of resolution. I also knew that even though Njeri protested, she knew what she had to do. And that eventually she'd do it.

Now I was in two dimensions. I couldn't make Njeri my problem. She wasn't. And I had to detach from her so that I could continue in my search. I had to find the connections I was looking for. Perhaps Njeri had provided some of them for me. For some reason, I felt vaguely certain that the other answer had to do with love. I would soon discover that story from the rising of the waves within me, waves of desire, lines of sacred geometry, the heart and wings and hidden smiles from eyes that were quiet fire.

"Do it," I said. "Just don't quit–you are unique, you know." And I could feel myself becoming distracted, wandering away into my present time which merged surrealistically with the old other time and with images resurrecting Lars' mystery. How strange it felt to be shuttered in and out of different time-space zones almost at the same instant. It felt as though I was stationary, but the past and the future were present all at once in different places in my psyche.

Or perhaps should I tell her to give it all up because it didn't matter anyway. The world may be contained in a "grain of sand" but not everyone could swallow that grain. I knew Njeri more than anyone else could. Yes, she was my problem, no concern, again–also a responsibility in some way. So I ventured, "Njeri, this is perhaps the last thing that I'll tell you. Drop out, you're too good for this place. Move on."

She gave me a look of disbelief, but strangely a cloud had lifted. I added, "this is another prison…get out before you… this…all this eats you." She shook her head, mumbled a "goodbye" and "how odd you are" and left. I had failed her in some way.

I looked at her walking down the hallway and wondered whether she had noticed anything strange about me. After all this time, I was from another time. I then busied myself with the task at hand–to find that fragment. I had left something behind, and I needed it in order to allow my destiny full rein.

I looked down at my hands only to find in them a small notebook in which I had the addresses of two men and one woman, each very important to my life, for each knew three different stanzas of a poem that contributed to my poem. That poem was about my passage, and in the turning of my world when I had disappeared, I had lost my one and only copy. Not one with a Xerox memory, I could only retrieve phrases here and there. The complete work was lost to me. I needed that poem because it was the passport to my future. That poem was about the state of being, about love, a love that is universal, complete, ever-flowing, unchanging, constant. And delicious. Was that last stanza for Lars?

Suddenly, I was no longer in my college office but in my other newer office at the Center for Visionary Arts where I'd met with the three most important people in my life. Just a thought could transport me where I needed to be. I hoped that I had done the final good deed for Njeri, but I knew I had not satisfied her–yet the essay she had turned in was remarkable. And she had returned to her same old life, suppressing her gifts.

I opened the notebook, wondered why it was still there. Of course, because I was there, am here, returned to my this body in this human time. And Nick's image floated in the space between my eyes and the page.

Nick Singh Jardin

I was looking through a telescope, a 1971 Christmas present to me from a friend who believed everyone must study the sky and know the designs up there, for they affected magnetically our lives on earth. I was playing with the instrument not at night, but on a horribly hot day, so much so that my eyes glazed over with moisture. Suddenly a bright light flashed in my vision, blinding me momentarily. I regained my composure and aimed my telescope pivoting it around to find something interesting when all of a sudden I caught myself staring at a large TV screen. There was Howard Beale shouting, "I'm as mad as hell and I want you to know it." It seemed he was talking to me. I shut my eyes. Clearly my zoom had turned to its max. I couldn't hear the words, but I could, I mean, a scene like that. Couldn't forget it 22 years later, (or 122 years later – what time zone was I in?). But my ears were becoming attuned and no sooner than I recovered from the shock to my eyes, then my ears went ricocheting for sounds.

"Hey for Pete's sake," yelled a loud gruff voice. A man got up even as this cute and grungy terrier bound right out of the window yapping his head off to announce the arrival of two carloads of people. Nine got out of the cars. Nick peeped out. I moved away behind the curtains in my room. Of course, he couldn't see me, but I could see him and I felt that because I could, that he could. I looked at him then carefully and felt as though I'd known him before or would know him again, which felt as though I'd know him because I'd known him before.

In a moment his living room was spilling over with guests. Joviality permeated the room like a bottle of fresh champagne recently uncorked. Up here in my space, I crouched. It was hot and so bright I had to be careful not to let my telescope walk into any spot of bright light. I then sensed that Nick would become a friend, one to own a piece of the poem that I have now returned to retrieve so that I can plan for my initiation.

Born to parents who rejected old ways, it was natural that Nick was a pioneer, eons ahead of his time. Nick Singh Jardin was a man with a vision, an educator, whose dream was to establish such schools that nurture the very essence of the individual. Such men were important to society; unfortunately, they weren't heard. They had power and that was threatening. And Nick wasn't one to impose anything onto others. He had learned the fine art of stepping back and watching others tumble over their overalls and titles. He'd smile. I had to go and see him back in that time.

Nick Jardin was raised in a small town in South East France to an Indian father and French mother. His father Soma P. Singh was a writer who had studied and taught at the Sorbonne, having left India at age 22 in 1920 in the heyday of swinging royalty albeit under colonial rule. A descendent of royalty, he abdicated all such power and luxury for the life of an intellectual creative wanderer. Despite all the various bribes from his family he remained true to his ideal. He studied literature at the Sorbonne, and soon after got a job teaching. There he met Mathilde Jardin, an older woman and his student.

Mathilde taught yoga at the Institut de Philosophie Indienne in Paris. After two sessions of yoga and three discussions of philosophy within one week, they were madly in love with each other. In two months, they were married. Soma held a secret passion for the poetry of the Vedas and Mathilde responded to that. Soma loved to talk about the Caravaka principles and the existentialists, drawing some similarities in the two schools of thought.

Basically, he was a modest man, simple in his attire, simple in his eating habits and always a twinkle in his eyes. He was very gentle with Mathilde, very appreciative of her philosophical approach to life. She grounded him, and he needed that. In turn he was always very protective of her. She was made of strong fibre, was secure in her femininity, and also embraced his protectiveness with grace and wisdom. It was the right way.

It wasn't long after they were married, about two years later, that they conceived their first child. Suraya Claire was born to them on April 1, 1926, a spring child with large hazel green eyes, black hair and a complexion like golden light, like olives kissed by a gentle sun. She had a small pretty mouth and she smiled often, yet there was a sense of melancholy about her that neither Soma nor Mathilde could quite understand. She was just a baby. And one so wise as though born outside of her time, whenever that is or was supposed to be.

Suraya would frequently gaze out the window over the tops of trees that laced Paris streets leading one's gaze at a bit of sky and at wrought iron baroque balconies with sculptures. Mathilde wondered what thoughts floated in her little girl's mind. At almost two years old, Suraya would do yoga with her mother, and with her quiet assurance, she was always ready to laugh with her father's playfulness. Their life together was braided with a quiet deference for life, an understanding of each other's uniqueness and a respect for the deeper contemplative space in each other.

When she turned two, Suraya fell very ill. She lay almost grey and blue one night chilled with fevers and no one knew quite what was the problem. Several doctors visited and discussed various theories, but none could reach a consensus. In short, they were baffled. At the same time, Mathilde was pregnant with her second child and very worried about her first. Soma was beyond grief; he wouldn't get out of her sight. He nursed her day and night with Mathilde who continued with her daily regimen as best as she could.

One evening, exhausted and needing some air, he stepped out. He hadn't gone to work in one week. He was walking down Boulevard St. Michel towards the fountain blindly, not caring where he walked. He crossed the Seine, the water was rushing by like his chaotic thoughts in a mad frenzy. Suddenly he found himself by the Cathedrale de Notre Dame. He stopped in front of the friezes and the one that caught his eye was of a male figure holding his head in the crook of his arm. He stared at it though it made no sense to him, but he started silently to repeat the word "*Chinnamasta*" and stepped backwards. He almost stepped into Pierre, a very old man with sharp eyes, long white beard. Dressed in a long black overcoat, Pierre was bent over and walked with a cane. Pierre had been looking at Soma for a while and seeming to recognize the man, he said softly, "Soma Singh? Prince Soma Singh?"

Soma stared at Pierre. Pierre continued, "Delhi, Bikaner. I was your father's visiting physician." In a flash, Soma saw the picture. Some connection was made at that moment. And he responded, "Yes, yes, Dr. Rimbaud. By god, it's been some 15 years now, I would not have recognized you as readily as you did me." "Well, I've changed more than you have naturally Soma. I heard you were here teaching at the Sorbonne. Such a hearty rebel you are. I am happy to see you. Brings back old good memories. But you don't look so well, what is the matter? Is there something that I can do?" Pierre asked.

Soma told Pierre about Suraya's illness. "It is of the spirit, not of the body, Soma. There is a general illness in the world. Have you not seen it, or heard of it? It is like a spiritual plague. People are dying. That is why the doctors were baffled. They won't let go of their pills nor will they acknowledge that illness is of the spirit," said Pierre with serious concern.

"But she's so young. Why must she suffer from a spiritual plague? I don't understand," responded Soma.

"When you arrived here a few minutes ago, I watched you. You went straight for the friezes without really thinking of where you were going. And the one that caught your attention was that one over there (Pierre points) the one without the head. And when you saw that you started. It reminded you of *Chinnamasta*—did it now?"

"Actually yes, how did you know?" Soma was amazed and wondered if Pierre had indeed read his mind.

"What does *Chinnamasta* mean to you? Is it not the headless *Kali*, the destruction of the ego, the image of righteousness, the process of clarifying and crystallizing the spirit in a new dimension? In the dimension of light," Pierre reminded Soma of things he had allowed to lie buried.

"You know Pierre, Suraya is extremely sensitive. She has this look of melancholy, as though she knows that the world was always doomed, yet she laughs so readily. Or does she just humour me? Is she a gift or a lesson or both?" Soma became silent. The night sky was turning colder and quieter. Soma began to feel a new quiet enter him as well. "Mathilde would be broken if anything happened to Suraya," he added.

"Hmmm...I think you would be more so. She embodies your

philosophy and poetry, Soma—the very reasons for which you left your family, refusing the crown. The very reason for which you stick to your principles and live a simple life. There is no simple life, of course," Pierre said, looking at Soma. "When I was with your father, I saw how broken he was by your refusal to stick with tradition, but a part of him knew it was better for you....When your mother died, it seemed to be all over for him. But he stuck it out. Sulekha was the next pillar in that house."

"*Chhoti behan*...my little sister," mused Soma, noting the similarities between Suraya and his little sister. His troubled face was no less in anguish an hour later as they reminisced about old times, the father's court, the religious ceremonies conducted to *Kali* and *Durga*, the religious holidays, for his thoughts returned to Suraya and Mathilde. He felt almost guilty for being away so long.

Pierre looked at Soma and said, "I'll come up and check on your little girl. They walked in silence listening to the clapping of feet on the pavement. A carriage passed by once in a while. It was nearing 11:00 p.m. They turned a corner and were at the entrance to the building of Soma's flat. They walked up the dark dimly lit stairs to the flat. Mathilde had seen them through the window, so she opened the door to let them in. She smiled softly at Pierre to welcome him in. Soma then took Pierre straight into Suraya's room.

The girl lay in silence, still somewhat blue and chilled with fevers. Pierre took one look at her, sat down by her feet, held her little feet in his hands and went into a meditation after gesturing to the parents to leave. An hour or so later, he came out to the living room where Mathilde and Soma sat together, Mathilde had dozed off in Soma's arms. She awoke on hearing Pierre's step. "Is she all right?" Mathilde asked.

"Take her out of the city. It's strangling the life out of her. Go away. Go south where it is still fresh. That's what she needs," he said to them. "That child, too, that's coming....Make preparations." Mathilde looked at him with a question in her eyes. "She'll be okay. She told me." He left it with a finality that he wouldn't say more. With that he quietly left the flat, promising to see them soon.

In two weeks when they were ready to leave, Suraya had become better though she was a little weak. Soma had resigned his job at the Sorbonne but would continue to do research for them. Mathilde was ready to leave, her strength gave the family a new vigor.

They moved to a small town in South East France near Avignon and made their home in a compact, five-room house with an attic and a basement. A more countrified life began for them and the adjustments were hard, specially for Soma who rather relished the stimulation of a teaching job. So he took to writing, while Mathilde started to teach the piano at a local school. Suraya recovered to become a quiet child with pensive dreamy eyes, who enjoyed playing in the garden and listening to music, particularly the flute, which she would learn to master later in her life.

After a long day of words and music, both Soma and Mathilde decided to recoup by sipping herbal infusions and got talking on their favorite subject, the definition of the self. Much had happened to change Soma's ordinarily childlike belief in the serendipitous order of events, but he hadn't lost his playfulness. A yoga adept, Mathilde had become somewhat skeptical, perhaps only outwardly so. It was even as they were questioning and arguing about the moment of conception as the birth of the self, when Mathilde felt the labor pains in her belly. After that it happened very fast. Soma called out to their neighbor Marianne to fetch the doctor, and Suraya sat quietly in the corner watching what was going on.

The doctor arrived an hour later. By then Mathilde was in intense pain. Soma sat holding her hand and stroking her head. He suggested to Suraya to go and play with Andre next door, but she sat where she was.

Nick was born on October 12, 1928 five hours later, making him two and a half years younger than Suraya. Nick had a shock of dark curly hair, and light brown almost amber eyes, and he grinned a lot. He was a healthy baby and loved to eat as was evident from the way he eagerly sought Mathilde's breast without any fuss.

It was in Avignon that the two children grew up and went to school. The eclectic and intellectually invigorating environment in which the two children were raised gave them both a far reaching and sensitive view of the world. Nick spent a lot of time with the village children and from his observations of human behavior, he learned to create games for them to challenge their minds and wit.

Together, Suraya and Nick also built model cities. Watching them play lead Soma to think that Nick would be a pioneer architect. But Nick displayed tremendous insight into human behaviors and patterns, how people learn, think and act. Not only was he curious about the way people acted, but he was also deeply compassionate. Mathilde would wonder at the little child's natural capacity to help others and be kind. Nick's gentleness and sensitivity made him a favorite among the townsfolk, specially the elderly.

Their childhood passed normally. Both children were blessed with wondrous gifts, a supreme love of nature and a healthy curious mind. By the time the war broke out, Soma had published two novels and three books of poetry. His first novel dealt with the nature of being combining his inquiry of *Carvakas* and the existentialists; his second novel (semi-autobiographical) was aimed at defining individual and communal culture and about the integration of cultures and its impact on civilization. Mathilde had successfully begun a yoga school in the remote French town.

Nick had been taciturn about the war years. He was at that time only about 9 years old when the war broke out in 1939. All he really talked about was the strength and support of his parents in those fearful times. Luckily for them, they were able to go away to India for the latter part of the war. When they returned there was nothing left of the old Avignon as they had known it. People had left, had gone away, had died.

They returned to India. Suraya and Nick were sent to study in Santiniketan, the school established by Rabindranath Tagore, a visionary, artist, writer and educator who earned the Nobel Prize in 1913. Having completed their studies at Santiniketan, Suraya would study to become a mystic healer and herbologist, and Nick at 18, came to the U.S. to continue his studies. So we met in 1972 at the Center for the Visionary Arts, where I had decided to take more classes.

I had known him for about eleven years now before I was transported from our known dimension to another one. He always had visitors thronging his house. I frequently gazed through my telescope. Loved to see things in faraway places. I put down the telescope and walked over to his house hoping that his guests wouldn't notice me. The little terrier wouldn't be fooled. It's the way of the dog. That sweet loyal little mutt. Suddenly I found myself wondering what Lars was up to. He had opened his soul to me one day. Since then everything had changed. I felt his aura checking me out. I suppose mine did the same. We aren't always aware of these aura meanderings, until the messages in our bodies feel different, bring a new awareness.

"Nick," I whispered through one window, knowing that he couldn't hear me. I could see him standing by the end of the living room, talking to a cherry-haired woman in a purple suit. His back was to me, but his face was reflected in an ornate gilt-edged mirror that graced the far wall and faced the window where I stood. So, of course, I could see his face in the mirror and he could see mine at a slight angle. I put my finger over my lips to shush him and slid away from view to the trees by the side of the house. A few minutes later he came out with a glass of lemonade. Those June days were always hot.

"Amiel, what in god's name are you doing here?...Who..? How did you get here?....You're a ghost?" Nick asked.

"No...I'm not a ghost, Nick. Here feel me," I put out my hand. "I'm the same old Amiel, Nick."

But Nick could not do more than stare, for what seemed like hours.

"Nick, I died or, more aptly, disappeared. Remember? Well, I suppose I am in various states of consciousness now and it's not a problem from where I come. In that time, space, consciousness conundrum....Don't look at me like that. I'm okay. Look...," but I was interrupted by Nick who stared at me perplexed and then caught me by the arm to lead me further away from the house to the garden. We went to a space by the pond well hidden from the house and the guests.

"Amiel, what are you talking about? You're rambling."

"Oh Nick. Well, nothing. Look I need to talk to you...Oh it is so good to see you...," we looked in silence at one another, and I continued. "Nick, your book on the sacred laws of wisdom. The poem you used. Mine. I need the original, the papyrus on which I wrote with blood. There's a fragment I can't remember. I need it. Where is it?"

"Can I get this straight?" He stood tall with a silver-edged mien and stared at me. I think it finally hit him what was happening. It was only three years ago on his birthday that I had given him the poem. Or he had taken it from me, just as he would have wanted to take everything from me. And I would have gladly gone with him, but for something that kept holding me back. He liked to believe it was Lars. It was and it wasn't. Lars just happened into my life and that was wondrous. But Nick had his own place. We had much to share, yet that little unnameable something didn't make it happen. I suppose our friendship was stronger than any other relationship between us could have been.

"Nick," I whispered. "It's still just me."

He sighed deeply. "Up to your tricks again." He smiled. "Tell me all."

So I did. As much as I could tell him. He filled me in with the work he had done in the last three years that we had not seen each other. "Nick, here is a school that the wise ones built. It is an integrated system. Like the one we used to talk about. It's a lifestyle. Citizens of the school wake up early and perform their communal duties, caring for the fields, or the buildings. Whatever it is. Teaching the young ones in their homes. Then they take their classes. All coursework is integrated, holistic, a gestalt experience of mind, body, and soul. Wish you could see it, Nick. Pure math, science, art, ecology, the spirit, music to move mountains and the tiniest grain of sand. That's how they learn to play music, with the understanding of the tiniest particle of sound and atom. Rarefied, refined. They glow. That's where you belong."

He smiled, his eyes wrinkling as only his could. "So will you take me back?...Amiel, I, too, built a small place, only under someone else's name. Focus on metaphysics, art, hard science and the care of the body...Speaking of which whatever happened to Lars?"

"Oh...Lars," I smiled trying to hide the delight in my eyes. "I don't know. You tell me. He was your favorite protege."

"He has the fragment you are looking for," Nick looked gravely into my face. I began to feel uncomfortable. This was going to take more courage than I thought I had. "He's older now," added Nick. You can choose the time when you want to see him. I could read Nick's mind clearly. He didn't say much. What he wanted to say rested below the surface of the words. Lars was part of the mystery that I had returned to bring back for the next stage in my journey. And I was almost anxious about the "delicious," like fine alchemized sheets of energy floating in and through my body, or through ours.

"So Nick tell me about the school. Is it the culmination of our plans and design? That grand building and campus that we drew again and again?"

"Well, on a smaller scale, but it is beautiful. It's in the Taos valley. Students learn to do various kinds of meditation. That's how the morning begins for them. Then they take the classes that interest them. A lot of hands on learning. There's a lot of open space around the buildings. Schedules are open, flexible. After a year at the school, students make their own schedules. They run the school as well.

"At dusk they conduct rituals. They dance. Tell stories. Play. Time for self-enhancement is the key. They have it. Learning to be in the body is so essential. The ultimate intricately designed temple of the soul. Not to be desecrated," Nick paused at my expectant look. "Do you want to see it?"

Of course I did. I wanted everything all at once. I just didn't know how much time I had over here. The time factor was different back where I had come from, but here it became an odd and uncomfortable constraint, a lesson in being fully present. I knew we'd go somehow. I just wondered why Nick wasn't there teaching by his presence. He was the finest educator the world had ever known, or so I thought. As though reading my mind, Nick looked at me and said, "I go there frequently. Students visit me off and on. I'm here a lot to raise money to keep the school going. Private funds. You see, mostly it runs like a co-op. Fees are minimal."

I reached out and embraced Nick closely. "I miss you Nick," I mumbled. He held me. I wanted to cry. Just a little.

As always, his patience and gentleness calmed me, made me feel I'd really come home. I have so many homes I thought. And now I've returned here on a mission.

Just then one of his guests called aloud for Nick and stepped out onto the verandah to look for him. Nick pushed me behind the bushes and said to wait there, to not move. It was rather late; I didn't realize how long we'd talked. I overheard the guest saying that people had begun to leave. I smiled caught in the shadows of the bushes trying to be as quiet as possible. That was Timbo, Nick's buddy and favorite tormentor, self-proclaimed arch actor and trickster of the gods. Loveable fellow really. But I must not step out. That would create quite a sensation. I was supposed to have died. Well, yes. In a sense I had.

    I suppose that would have been the right time to visit his school in Taos. But I really wanted to see it with Nick. I started to think about Lars. His hands, so pliant and deft. His calm and assured gait covering his slight limp; his eyes, quiet fire. I breathed deeply as my thoughts drifted to Lakshmi.

    "Where the prophets dwell, there shall I go/ Where they dream there shall I dream/ What they dream of, that shall I become..." I was softly reciting these lines to the swish of the breezes through the treetops when Nick came by in silence. His friends seemed to have left.

    "Lars. That's Lars' poem, isn't it? When do you want to see him?" Nick queried.

    "No, that's Lakshmi's poem. And Nick….before I see Lars, I need to see Lakshmi. Where is she?" I remembered. My little notebook was old, pages were torn, faded and even lost. I couldn't have found Lakshmi. I remembered her home, not how to get there.

    "I'm going to see her next week. She's ill. Can't say when. I can take you with me."

    No no, I couldn't wait that long. I smiled at the division of time into days and weeks. And our eternal wait to receive rewards. The twist and tussle of making things happen in the right time and the stressing over it. In the other world, it was different. I can't quite explain how. Not now.

    I looked at Nick tenderly eyeing his sideburns, his gentle eyes. I knew he was working out how to leave early so that he could take me to see Lakshmi, who lived a couple hour's drive out of the city in a wild and rugged canyon that looked purple in the setting sun, whose highlights brought fiery edges to the tops of trees and shrubs.

Lakshmi

    Early the next day, Nick and I set out for Twilight Canyon. I was still somewhat perplexed with my interaction with Njeri. It felt very strange to be back in the old time, in his old blue rusted Ford truck, on the road to see Lakshmi. The sun slaked its way on the thirsty dusty plains, and the shadows began to grow harsher. It was on such a day that I had taken the plane to visit friends in Nepal and the plane had disappeared.

"What's on your mind?" asked Nick peering into the harsh light, looking for the turn into the canyon.

"Just this. How to maintain sanity and balance in a rushing world of pressures and deadlines. Where everyone in your life is working out his/her own trauma and you are picking it all up. It affects you so you can't function in the ways that you wish and do the things that you believe you ought to be doing. How?"

"No one has the answer to that one. Remember Rene? Child of incest, torture. Why do people torture those that they believe they love? Why does a man beat his wife and then sleep with her? How can people be this way?" Nick asked.

"I don't know. I do know somehow that living with some kind of harmony is possible. I don't know how we can get there in this stage of our evolution," I mused and thought of the place where I had been with the wise ones.

The principles of love are simple, yet so hard to manifest. Receiving, allow. Fragments, just fragments float in my mind.

"If only we could see the core and function from that knowledge, bring that to our daily existence into matter and know that when we connect with another we are in a sacred space that binds us in that moment...forever. We know for having seen and been there."

"Amiel, you couldn't ever live in your body could you? Even your erotic poetry is in ether," Nick noted.

"Well, that's the way it is with me," I grinned, wondering, with a strange disquiet, about Lars. And saddened that I hadn't quite understood my body—its need to rest and be harmonized by the laws of nature. All that running around.

Now I understood what Nick had known all along, that the body is the landscape of the soul and its journey. It is in the body that we experience the ultimate bliss. This through right work, right living, right eating, right loving, right coupling. That the laws of the universe and of nature require us to procreate as well, to unite divine essence into the world; the coupling itself as the divine act makes that possible. This is part of the evolutionary process.

We stopped for breakfast at a wayside inn, ate in silence except for the intermittent buzzing of flies. The sun beaming from its girth had slowed things down. The inn keeper tried her best to be present and made us pancakes and juice. Fresh carrot-parsley juice so far out in the canyon. A couple of other customers sat either reading a newspaper, or just looking out at the few shrubs of green in the stark glare. A woman with a child who wouldn't sit still. A man with a pot belly and pants barely hiding a belly button. A long-haired young man with impatient eyes and a restless spirit.

"Amiel!"

"Hmm, yes," I responded.

It was time to go. We neared Lakshmi's house. Even from a distance I could see her sitting in her verandah dressed in white muslin. Stately, calm, wise. What went on in her mind few were privy to. Her husband had died a few years ago. She had grieved for some time, then had returned to her work in the university showering us with her usual sparkle of mischief from her vivid green eyes.

We reached her house and were met with disbelief and warmth. "Haven't seen you in years my dear." Then she looked over at Nick and bid him wait in the living room, as she bustled me inside to her inner chamber. She stared at me silently, she knew what I wanted. "I've heard things about other lands," she began. "Is it to such a place that you've disappeared? How did you do that?"

"What have you heard?" I asked.

"Oh, things. Some people believe that this is all a trick. But I know better. Why...do you not feel that you belong there?...Or are you not ready...Not ready to go there yet?" she gave me a cryptic smile. How much did she know?

I wondered if her questions were a trick. Then she silently bent down and from under a table drew out a small red basket and handed it to me.

"When we walk along the ridges of pain and look into the shadows, we see shades of blue. When we accept that pain and look into the sun, we see our souls as pillars stand upright in pride and fortitude. Shades of gold with swirls of green. And then does descend the Goddess of love with palms turned up offering her peaches for the srength of our suffering. And the Goddess of love returns to the ashes every night only to keep returning to heal us lest we forget."

Lakshmi motioned with her finger for me not to say anything, held my face with her two hands and said, "We've never parted, and we never shall."

That was a brief meeting. Teary-eyed, I nodded, we embraced and I stepped into the verandah to take in the freshness. Nick spent some time with Lakshmi going over school business. He promised to see her very soon again and we left.

I thought I would never see her again, but I was wrong. She did show up one day two years later and that was the last time. But the first time we met was 18 years ago, when I was a student in the Center for the Divine Arts. I wasn't sure what I was doing there, dabbling in one thing then another. First art, then poetics, then mythology. Everything was so intertwined for me that it was really difficult to let go of one. And that was the problem as well. My desire to study Sanskrit led me to sign up for a class with Dr. Prakash Dondy; but it was Dr. Lakshmi Baraka who showed up. It was under her tutelage that I accepted my interests in many things, but I also learned to bring them to balance and focus. Mythology with a focus on the arts. For image was it. It's the image that we keep in our minds when we pray, when we love, when we remember. It is the image that we desire and desiring remember—it is the image through which we remember the divine. So image making and unravelling became my forte and passion. The seed of thought itself, the beginning and the end. But as I was to learn later, there is no end, only a continuum.

Lakshmi, herself, was a poet. She'd come from Lithuania via the German detention camps, and having made it here, she met and married a man from Ethiopia. Assefa Baraka was a Sufi mystic and a medical doctor. They complemented each other very well. Their marriage was based not on the wild imaginings of romantics nor of those waiting for the right one to appear, but knowing each other and making each other right. Moreover, there was a deep love and respect between them. They believed that they each had endured the political struggles in their respective situations so that their paths might cross. Some force of karma, of fate.

Together they had one son whom they named Peter. Lakshmi acquired her name from a woman in the detention camp who wanted to name her daughter Lakshmi. The woman had died mysteriously one night and Elemi, out of some feeling of compassion or camaraderie adopted the name. It stayed. It turned out to her advantage to use the name Lakshmi instead of Elemi which, being common, was so easily recognized.

When she reached the US, she was briefly Lakshmi Ygor before she met Assefa at the university where he taught medicine. Herself a renowned scholar in her hometown, Lakshmi was assistant to the dean of humanities at the same university as Assefa. She continued her research in languages and the history of consciousness.

About her life in Lithuania I learned little, for not many people really knew much about her past. All I gleaned from close associates was that she had been raised on a farm. She had one brother who, as it turned out, was mentally handicapped as a result of an accident. That left her to shoulder the responsibilities of the home, since her mother was away a lot. But Elemi loved to read, so she also went to college.

She had an uncle who encouraged her interests and brought her books and music. After graduating from university and publishing several articles in scholarly journals and one book, she had a job teaching East European and African literature.

Then the war uprooted her family, her village, the neighboring villages—the country was in turmoil. Her parents were taken prisoner while she was out one afternoon. When she returned, she saw the devastation and, hiding behind trees, she managed to be safe and find other villagers. But not for long. They were all taken in, shoved into trucks, taken to detention camps.

A few times she opened up and told me of her life in Lithuania, of her first love in the village, that he'd bring cherry blossoms for her hair, that they'd sing together (he was a flautist) that they had plans to live in the big city. Shortly before the war, he fell mysteriously ill and died. No doctor could figure out what happened. She decided to never marry, but later events proved otherwise.

She told me of the stories that people told each other and their children, stories handed down from generation to generation that kept alive the culture, the passions, and dreams of the people. All that was held sacred was desecrated by the madness of one man and his cohorts. Then her face would become clouded as she hid distant memories from me. Suddenly, the shadows would lift and she'd mention the way the sun shone through the desolation of the winter bringing color to her home town and to the faces of its inhabitants.

Indeed, she was an inspiration to many of us. It was from her that I learned to connect with Mother Earth, with the richness of my Indian heritage, for she illustrated layers of meaning in our stories. It's true that she seemed aloof and unapproachable, but when she did communicate, she was very generous with information. Her life was a book of knowledge and wisdom. Moreover, she taught us with clarity and compassion. We worked for 15 years together and I'd still go to her for counsel on important subjects.

It is also Lakshmi who both guarded me jealously and scolded me vociferously for not being diligent and disciplined with my work. She pushed me to perform beyond my limits; she made me stretch my limits; she made me angry. But she made me grow in ways that no one else had done. She was the one who encouraged me to work on the plans for the school that both Nick and I dreamed of, where we would teach and come in contact with people like Sita, Lars and many others, the promise of the future. For education or knowledge is the key to unravelling our destinies. She was the one to make me work on my poem—"...blue-gold silent laughter in winds/ promise of seeds from the eye of the sun/ to our feet..."—and the fragment that I have come to retrieve.

I have begun to feel of late that it is not any fragment I have come for, but to fulfill a grander purpose. I don't know yet what that is. Time will tell. Is it that I have come back to learn how to love? To learn that "nothing is complete/and that is to love." Am I a fragment waiting to be whole?

In the meanwhile, I am perplexed at Lakshmi's statment "we've never parted, and we never shall." Little did I know then that, yes, we would meet again. Later. After my mission was done. After I had been to see Lars. That then would be our last meeting.

Lars

The next day I was on my way to see Lars. In the red basket was a peach that Lakshmi had given me and some almonds. Oh, how I began to crave a mango. All the world must be contained in a mango, the seeds of all the fruits.

When Lars had first shown me his soul, his eyes had become lit by a quiet cool fire. After that he'd become shy, nervous. Well I had been the teacher again. Perhaps he should have made it with Kira. We all had similar ideas of how the world ought to be–with Lars, Sita and Nick and others as the most aware of and accepting of reality. And I? Well. I was given to fantasies and utopian dreams. I was the one out there waiting for the perfect worlds to emerge from some fantastic realm. The world is harmony and we have to put people back into the world. I believed that. I am glad they laughed at me sometimes.

Now meeting Lars again was inevitable. I was almost not prepared for what would happen when we met.

He lived in a remote town between the mountains and the ocean, spanning the layers of fire and water and mists. When I arrived at his house, he was planing wood for a table top. How perfect, I thought as I stood aside watching. Practical. Down-to-earth. Good with his hands. I always respected a man who could build things. I stood outside watching him. Slowly, he lifted his head. I could see he had made a place for himself away from grey walls and plaster, away from cheese ceilings. This was idyllic. He knew how to live and be in his center.

Lars Brahman had come from a long line of builders, middle class people, from the heart of Denmark who had emigrated to America at the turn of the century and settled in Bethel, Maine. There they continued their work as builders.

The fifth of seven children, Lars was the inconspicuous one, quiet, unassuming. Even as a child he was used to being on his own; he'd wander off into the woods by himself; he'd sit in his room and play the flute; he'd make no fuss over his food. He was the dark-haired one, unlike most of his siblings, and somewhat more frail looking than the others.

He was more like Arin, his sister, seven years older, the third child. They got along well. It isn't that they did much together, it's that they understood each other. The oldest sibling, a sister, had left home at age 18 to study in New York; the second, a boy, was an outdoors sporty sort, more physical than the others and his goal was to join professional baseball; then Arin who was quiet, warm, and friendly; then Jana, the house clown, playful, nutty, mischievous. After Lars came two boys a year apart, the older of the two was but two years younger than Lars. It was a complex situation, but Lars' parents being simple family-oriented people, spent a lot of time involving group activities.

Family dinners were an important ritual in the wood-panelled dining room furnished with an old heavy rustic wooden table and chairs. They ate home cooked meals. Even the bread and butter were made at home. Lena, the mother, made everything from scratch. It is hard to imagine any one person doing all that work. But Lena was quite the earth mother who nurtured and provided, while Elmar worked on building projects to bring home money. It was a stable family built on the values of cooperation and mutual respect, though not without its weaknesses as well—that being that equal attention to the kids was not always possible.

It was after one very active day at school, in the forest and one cosy family meal that Lars went to his room and settled in for the night, as did the other children. He hadn't been very well of late, but characteristically had kept silent about it. The following day when everyone trooped down for the day, Lars was missing. Arin came up to check in on him and found him unconscious with high fever. That was the turning point in his life. It seemed that he had come down with a bad case of meningitis. Luckily for the family, their doctor was very very good and reliable. He had treated three such cases before and cured one.

Through the next few nights Arin and Lena sat with Lars, holding cold compresses. At that time, Lars was only nine years old. One night Lars was unconscious. That drove Arin mad with anger and fear. This was her little brother. She would not leave his side. It wasn't until he opened his eyes and Arin was assured that he would be all right that she even went to sleep. Apparently, the worst was over. Doctor Marten pronounced that Lars would live. They had to monitor him for some months for any possible brain damage. This only drew Arin and Lars closer. And everyone in the house began to be more aware of his presence and absence more. This made him sometimes uneasy, although nothing ever fazed Lars. He took everything in stride. He was present when they needed him to be present; he was in his own world when he needed to be there. The real change that came over him was that he became very focussed. Like his father he learned to work with his hands. He would be a builder. He would infuse the idyllic in his designs.

When he came to the Center for Visionary Arts, he was already a master builder. He came to further his studies in sacred geometry to enhance his sense of spaces. He came to be a part of the vision for the new world. He was a student of Nick Jardin for one year, and my mentee for that time as well. We developed a natural affinity and spent much time together, but we had never broached the subject of our attraction that hung like expectant stalagtites around us, wanting to be melted, tasted.

◆❖◆

As quietly as possible, I stood looking at him work. He lifted his head to look for some tool and in the slant of a ray, he caught my shadow by the tree. Squinting to see what had appeared in his gravelly driveway, he shaded his eyes with his hand and stepped out. I felt bound in an auric capsule where space stretched rarefied in the hand of eternal time.

He smiled his wondrous magical smile. I became a mush of atoms of light of energy. Of course, I was here to learn how to be contained in my body, I realized. Of course, I had returned to learn about love. He walked towards me, with a slight barely noticeable limp.

"Hello," I said, a safe innocuous greeting. Appropriate. He looked up from his work and stared for some moments before registering that it was me standing there. In front of him.

"Amiel? Ghost...? he ventured. I shook my head.

"This is a surprise. I thought you were gone. Aren't you a ghost?" he asked laughing but with a seriousness that belied humour.

"Yes, I am. No... it's lovely to be here, Lars." We stood still staring at one another. Then quietly and as cautiously, we walked towards the house which rested on the highest ledge, a promontory overlooking the ocean. We went to the edge and sat on a green bench, unsure of this new space between us and that which contained us.

"Hello Amiel," he said laughing, then looked at me and became still. "Look at me," he insisted. I swallowed my heart beats, but they stuck somewhere in my throat. We held up our hands and our fingertips touched ever so lightly, the way we used to do. Lifelines opened up coursing with wild energy focused somewhere beyond our will.

Struggling to surface, we breathed deeply and slowly bringing our bodies to balance.

"It is the light," he quoted.
"Eat the light," I replied.
"It is the fire."
"Burn with it."
"I am the light and the fire."
"The timbre of flowing water."
"The clashing of thunder and light."
"The conception and the gestation."

And then we became deathly still. "Lars, they didn't send me to bring anything back. I have it all. They sent me to complete the ritual of life. With you?"

"Who is they? What are you talking about?" he asked quietly if not more perplexed than Nick.

"Never mind," I replied. "Nick told me you have the fragment. That's what I came for."

"Fragment? I see you after aeons and you talk about a fragment that really has no bearing on how you and I are feeling right now." Seeing that I was stunned by his retort, he quickly added, "But you have it...in your mind," he said.

No, you are the whole and the fragment. I shivered slightly. "Lars, let's go in, I'm cold."

We went into the cottage. The inside walls were a light golden-peach, white, and blue. At late sundown the winds began to howl, and it became suddenly very very cold.

"Tell me more. What's new in your life?" I asked.

"New in mine? What about you? You disappear in a plane and aren't ever heard from again. Where did you go? And you haven't changed...I mean you tell me," Lars was shouting. Gone was the initial calm. "What do you know about the...about love or hate or anger or or anything at all? What do you know how it is to be left out in the raw cold all alone? I.. I...." He threw his hands up in the air, his face red with rage. "The world is a lovely space/ when your face is turned/ towards sunlight vistas..."

This did not sound like Lars, the Lars that I had known. Life's turns brings things into the open that remain hidden for too long. Suddenly, a shadow.

Clouds had gathered at an alarming rate, raging across the skies blacking out the twilight. I turned to look out the window. The ocean water was gushing round madly, a medley of whirlpools and torrential waterfalls. I looked back to see Lars sitting on his orange sofa. I went and sat beside him at an angle so that we were almost face to face. My eyes fell on a fragment framed in blue–"whose voices command/ the resonance of pure thought…"– on the wall beside images of his inventions.

"Lars, Nick said you had a child. Where is he? Where's Sita?" I asked.

He glowered at me and I wondered if I was out of place asking this. Or asking so quickly. He was right to be angry with me. After all I had run away once and then just disappeared. Here I was clutching at the sameness that I believed was perennial, but surfaces change.

"I'm sorry," I said, quietly.

"No, I'll tell you," he said very firmly. "You want to know. I want to tell you…After all…"

Silence hung like a thick curtain of black transparent velvet, with things softening around us, our breathing becoming more in synch.

"Over and out. It wasn't what it was meant to be. Wrong match. And you'd do better to keep out of the way…." He became quiet, then resumed talking. "It was my problem really. I wanted to feel that you were around so I could talk sometime. Just know. You who had seen my soul, you who knew, you who talked about… you walked away into the clouds. How did you do that?" Lars said, his anger and exhaustion turning giving expression to sarcasm.

"Stop that," I said sharply, feeling that I was being pulled into this without quite wanting to be there, yet knowing I couldn't resist it. And becoming confused. What was this mystery that I did not know how to read? What was Lars? Who was he? Who am I? Who was I? My confusion was not about him, but about me. My unresolved destinies.

I wanted to recall stories–I wanted to forget them.

Thunder rolled across the heavens, a spate of lightning lit up the wild sky, and rain started in a sprinkle only to turn into a torrent a few moments later. Lars got up to start a fire. I stood by watching, very aware of the intensity of the anger in the rainfall. Very aware of the soothing fire burning, crackling so close to me. Their sounds so similar, so similarly affective, quietening, slowing, throwing one into introspection. But now the cold was angry and the hot was soothing. I felt raw, caught stretched on a line in a vortex. I felt Lars behind me. Very slowly, he reached out and embraced me from behind. That was the signal for all control to dissipate even as the earth was washed away with rainwater outside.

Our kisses turned hunger inside out; we grasped at each other until there was nothing to grasp, and we were but one. The ocean too writhed on this blackest night with all its might heaving wave over wave unto wave under wave over wave, until desire and challenge rolled into one tight ball of extasy. Right there as I was leaving my body, he held me, he bid me stay. "Open your eyes," he commanded. I did. "Look at me," he commanded. I did.

The rain continued its raucous patter, the fire began to soothe away the rough edges that had hung around us scratching our surfaces into the deep chasm within.

Our hands were clasped by our sides, my legs wrapped around him. That's how we fell asleep, his body sprawled on mine. I didn't know when he got up and covered us with a comforter. I didn't know when he pulled the blinds down. I didn't know when the rain stopped. It was very early, the sun barely cracking open the sky when I stirred ever so slightly. His head peered up at me. His eyes pierced me again; our kisses were slow, gentle and lingering for what seemed like hours, and suddenly as though hitting the continental shelf, we surrendered to the mystical moon. Again we were in each other. Again I knew we were traveling to ancient forests and breathing in cedar and climbing the tops of the heavens and landing on the other side of the sun.

And this time when we came with each other, I knew some sacred act had been done. As only in the coupling of Shiva and Parvati, when consciousness travels in the nooks and crannies, the shadows in each other's body to seek the god or goddesses within. To seek them. To know them. Indeed, to become them. Pure rage! Pure love!

The divine essence was in our space and had now coagulated with a spark inside of me. Surely, I had conceived. I was as sure of this as Savitri when she won her husband back from Yama, Lord of Death. Savitri, the mother of evolutionary principles. Moving us towards the light.

It was all here, I realized with a joyous dread. The pain, the heartache, the sorrow, the anger, the anguish, the separation, the yearning, the tears, the uniting, the touch. Through all this, knowledge. Word fragments mattered not but the living poem. This loving, a continuum. And loving not mere joy, but the pain and fear of tearing the veils that keep intimacy at bay.

This was the beginning of the gestation. And the culmination of years of wondering, waiting, watching, being tentative.

We lay wrapped in crisp white sheets for quite a while, savoring the moments of each other's being, the fragrance of knowing completion. He lifted his head from my breasts and asked what had really happened all these years.

Finally, I told Lars the whole story. He had a right to know everything. "I was taken away in a plane load of people to Mahaloka, the next stage in our evolution. Lars, I don't know how I got there, but once there it was hard work for me at first. It was as though I felt very natural being there in the first place, it was everything I imagined a place to be, like we used to idealize, yet..I suppose I could hardly believe it.."

"But where is this place? How do you get there?" asked Lars.

"No maps exist for Mahaloka. You just have to know where it is and do what you have to do to be there. It's very distant from what we know here. Suffering has its place, it's internal and not inflicted from the outside by others. It is the suffering like dust that flies, and meandering finds its place to settle. Blameless, above...beyond judgement. Not that of inflicted pain and torture, of rapes, of killings, but in its more essential aspect. The memory and desire for the source. The knowledge of the source."

Lars murmured, "yes..stigmata movements in the body."

Nuzzling and nibbling his ear, I agreed, "something like that. Light needing space."

He lifted his head and looked at me thoughtfully, "light needing space. Doesn't it have its space...?

"Perhaps, the space to spread."

"Once light has found its path it cannot but spread, Amiel."

"Same with love, but that's all poetic. Here in this realm, it is easier to be obstructed and...deviant. Is that the word I want? Hmmm. I'm not so sure. But we can easily get caught in mirrors instead of going beyond. So if there is a bit of light, people are joyed by it...but also confused by it."

"Okay how is this?" and Lars held my lips in his mouth. Our arms spread out, our legs spread out like a coupling Da Vinci mandala in the most poignant still point. Our cerebrospinal fluid in sync, heart beat matching heart beat until nothing else existed. Light petals falling. We felt like we were light, we are, lifting in an ethereal embrace, blessed by each other, recognizing the source within...the body, this vessel.

My eyes filled with tears as I sighed deeply, breathing his essence into my bones.

"Lars?"

"Hmm, yes." Almost inaudible.

◆❖◆

We were walking along the mountain ridge early the next evening. The mists had lifted. The sun whose rays had been muted now sought us with a directness we hadn't seen or felt for some time.

The valley spread out below us. Large rocks sat with a quiet aplomb in this remote haven. Lars walked to a particularly interesting rock and felt it with his hands—large and beautifully shaped, marked with the toughness of labor. Work of love. He loved to work with his hands and he made the most unusual things. He was a master builder. Everything he touched transformed into a thing of beauty—all the polarities came alive; nothing in the human experience was short of reach for him.

Then why the reclusive lifestyle? He could really contribute to transforming society. He believed in the power of stillness to affect change. "Amiel, look at this. See the texture here...?" and he looked up at me.

I couldn't help but smile. He always made me smile, but at the bottom of my heart was a sinking flutter of fear, a tremor I hadn't felt in aeons, not ever in Mahaloka. I knew I had to commune with the Wise Ones. What if they wouldn't let me back? What if they wouldn't let Lars go with me? Had I found what they wanted me to find and complete?

Lars who was still looking at me saw the changes in my face. He stepped up and held my elbows. "Mirror mirror on the wall..."

"The mirror cracked from side to side... Well, I was just looking at you...wondering."

"Wondering what?" he asked his eyes twinkling.

"Don't know. Really. There. Here. Such different worlds. So where does that leave us?"

"You're not running away are you?" he asked, knowing full well I couldn't or wouldn't go anywhere.

"Lars. Lars...," I stopped. He was laughing at me.

"Wait wait wait... here hold your hand up to mine. Let's see if this works.....Now breathe deeply and allow yourself to merge here with me."

Very gradually, I could feel myself shifting time lines and disappearing. Then Lars suddenly jerked my hand back. Although he had started to shift, he didn't do it completely. Perhaps he wasn't ready for a complete transformation, but we'd make it soon.

I was in both realities all at once. Here I was with Lars. There I was with the Wise Ones strolling in raspberry fields. "Greetings Amiel. We were wondering if you'd ever return."

"Greetings, Satyamuni. Can I come back now?" They chuckled.

"Did you find what you were looking for?" asked Dhruva, the august sage.

"I'm not sure what you sent me back for. I found the poem..but that is not what you wanted me to bring back."

Manjusri smiled and pulled out a conch shell. She blew on it and handed it to me, "Call out on this on special occasions...Or if you wish to see me."

I received the conch from her and blew hard. Even Lars could hear that. He was holding onto the end of my shawl, so I could feel every movement of his. Present in this time-space continuum and feeling the light firing my being, I was sure that Lars too could feel what I was experiencing, and he could participate in the shift.

Manjusri saw my moving expressions and noted, "Yes, but not now. There's more that you two have to do."

"What?" I asked, unwillingly resigning myself to an unsettling and long period of searching, working and learning patience.

Dhruva stepped up to us with an expression of kind wisdom and amusement, "Your task, both of you, is to give the world an image, an expression of peace. That's all. Then you'll be here in a moment."

I laughed in disbelief, "An expression of peace?..." I could feel Lars tugging at my hand in some sort of affirmation. "Sure, we can do it," he said, as though it were the easiest thing to do in the world. The active principle of giving form. Do we need more books, stories, paintings? Do we need to create more? Do they lead us to clarity or to more confusion? Just more of everything, taken out of their natural elements and moulded into tools for us all. So that we lose natural contact with simplicity in our lives. But what else do we have? His clarity. Yes.

I felt a stirring within me. I knew it was something that I had wanted very much to do. Those were our plans in the Center for the Visionary Arts a long time ago. Nick, Lakshmi and I along with Lars and some others had talked about it. The school that Nick had established was continuing the work. I had of course disappeared. Lars had come away to this remote place and built his cottage. The memory of another reality struck me like a fine chord of light that penetrated my crown and landed me on my feet. I was to love the earth, more now because of Lars.

I bid the wise ones goodbye and returned, somewhat sorrowful, concerned, confused and taken aback. But Lars stood beside me, a figure of strength. Standing on a large deep rust rock, we embraced.

"Well," he said, "now what?"

"Now nothing. Let's go home."

"What do they look like?"

"Who? Manjusri and the rest?" Lars nodded. "Well, like us, only very vibrant with life and energy, full of vitality.. Eyes sparkling, skin glowing. Mmmm...well, somewhat less dense matter.. a light dense matter. There's a fluidity about their movements...and grace...

like swans gliding in the waters at dawn, unwatched, uninhibited. Wild. Free. Self-contained. Fiery. The fire that illuminates."

But I was troubled. Troubled by how we would achieve this grand illusion. And I wondered if there is a way to create images reflecting our higher selves and project them all over the world at the same time. Project the images and narratives not on screens, but on ethereal screens where they appear like magic. Is such a thing possible? Do we have the scientific know-how to make this happen? I thought if we could do such a thing, we could affect people the world over, in remote places as well, with images telling stories of wholeness, of light, of wisdom. And such images would re-ignite in all the virtue of joy—would not this be a blessing to us all?

♦❖♦

Lars and I left to visit with Nick at the Center for the Visionary Arts the following week. Firstly, we wanted to really just see Nick. We also wanted to know what work had been initiated to promote peace and mindfulness.

Nick was waiting for us when we arrived. "Amiel, you haven't disappeared yet, how come? Lars, are you keeping her on the earth? Welcome."

We walked around for some time. It was interesting to return to the center after what seemed like a lifetime; the unfamiliar impinged upon the familiar and vice versa. I had changed, yet I had also been there just the other day when I reconnected with Nick. But this visit was remarkably different. I had returned here with Lars. I wondered what it would be like had I never left.

Nick took us to an old building made of sandstone columns and flying buttresses, with carvings gracing the walls. We went in to the studios and laboratories where students were working on their art. A sculpture garden in the inner sanctum of the building served as the heart or the hearth where students on recess rested, talked, meditated. Bells and chimes hung in various places, bringing a charm so characteristic of this place.

It struck me how trapped we are in our very expressions of reality, of utopian ideals. Nothing is free from tension and conflict, competition and jealousy. We feel that we are freeing ourselves from traps by creating another story or sculpture, but we just walk from one trap to the next. Perhaps, we feel some awakening or freeing, but we fall right into another desire to create and to make something new. Our desire to create is not always for a kathartic effect, but to have some control over our lives, to give it meaning.

I stopped and looked around me, only to find that I was in a shaded space, surrounded by trellised walls. Neither Nick nor Lars was with me. I was alone, must have wandered off carelessly. Again. I felt that I was in some sort of time warp chamber, for all sounds seemed to echo from great distances, as though through layers of walls and spaces. But this place wasn't enclosed.

In the center was a small round dais. I sat down and shut my eyes momentarily. Sounds were far away and mumbled; I heard my name but thought it best to remain here, so they could find me, instead of me looking all over and getting lost, something that is second nature to me. Getting lost.

Delicately carved calligraphy surrounded the dais. One said, "We find ourselves in the mirrors we create." Another, "We must go beyond the mirrors that we create." "Life is not a reflection after all." "Life is the great stillness in the chaos." "Love is." "I am love and loving." A deep sadness permeated me. A flood of memories swept into my body, reawakening all the reasons why we become separate from ourselves and each other, reinvoking the angst over the horrors in the world and our collective history. The story of Njeri, her lovely sad face speaking to me her truth, her desperate truth: "You don't understand...it's not so simple as you make it out to be. You know... shit!" And, "Why can't you leave me alone and let me live the way I am supposed to?"

That was the real question: How are we supposed to live? Thank you Njeri, I said quietly in my mind. I hope I meant it. Footsteps sounded down the hallway although this space didn't seem as though it was part of another structure. I overheard Nick saying to Lars as their steps came closer, "...and this here is an extension, a sort of secret space, not easy to find. To find it you have to know it exists." I felt like a thief, an intruder.

Lars stood at the entrance. I looked at him and said, "It's not going to be easy, this work that we have to do...the teachings that we receive that we must pass on..."

"It's not meant to be easy, Amiel," he replied.

"...the structures that we must build, the expressions...it's not going to be easy..."

"No..it's not," he said.

"But we have to... for Njeri and others like her, for ourselves.... For forgiveness," I said.

"Yes...so why so despondent?"

His eyes missed nothing at all. "Just a moment of despair," I replied.

"You've traveled back all this way to be in despair?" he was serious.

I sighed and looked around and at him, realizing the beauty that Nick had created in his single-minded devotion to truth. And I looked at Lars wondering if I was betraying us all with my moment of fear. "This peace we are supposed to create and work for...what does it look like?"

"Okay, this is a good beginning—what does it feel like?" he said, a smile floating into his eyes—"you, the world within me/ is a sweet joy...." We watched Nick walk towards us with the sun setting far behind.

♦❖♦

One day, perhaps, we will be able to and ready to go to live with the wise ones in *Mahaloka*. Shruti, the child of both of our essences, could easily make it there.

She would be raised in places of wild wisdom: *Where rocks are craggy and powerful and winds sing. Where learning is as natural as the falling and tumbling of waterfalls. Where fragrances are mild and invigorating. Where children are not tortured by rigid school systems and forget their ability to be joyful and innocent. Where energy and essence are guided into creative fulfillment. Where the feminine and masculine principles each have their place in our psyches so that we complement each other and make a whole. Where our fires can bring us to balance through illumination.*

Where art is not a cold reflection of the meaningless but is a space for metamorphosis. Not grey walls but windows into the layers of self.

Where art is not a window or a mirror but Self manifest.

Epilog ~

Dear Readers ~

Thank you for participating in this journey with me until the final pages.

My attempt, in this book, is to crystallize my concept of Creative Resonance and extend its application to different areas of our life, as evident in the various chapters. My express purpose is then to take it out into the world through classes, workshops, poetry, art, and presence.

Naturally, this is all an ongoing process of co-evolution. We are here to assist one another to see the grandeur in all life and to respect its being here—just as it is. We are here to open doors.

Towards that end, I wish that you find your resonance in these pages and take with you whatever gift is in order for you here and now. I trust that you find for yourselves ways to be in complete creative rapport with your own core. I wish that you enjoy the poetry within you. I wish that you embody your innermost visions for what you want to become. I wish that you recognize that inner knowing and can assist your young ones to also manifest their greatest po(e)tential.

I trust the book opened doors for you, that the exercises helped you to journey deep into your sweetest core, healing untended areas along the way, transcending pain, and finding your joy. For now you will walk in your grace and in your greatness as a gift to humanity—as you are. You are a complete poem; therefore, each of you is a poet.

That would be, for me, an accomplishment—as you grow, so do I.

It is important for me to emphasize that this journey here is not about a spiritual practice or about enlightenment. It is about being completely present in our bodies, about actualizing ourselves to our fullest, about being aware of who we are individually and communally, so that we create our beauty in our external environments.

Finally, I acknowledge you and your magnificence.

Many many thanks.

With LoLiLa — "love, light, laughter."

Ambika Talwar

Appendix

"Nature uses only the longest threads to weave her patterns, so that each small piece of her fabric reveals the organization of the entire tapestry."
~ Richard Feynman

The Making of Golden Matrix Visions

One mid-December morning in 2002, I stood in my living room looking out the window—this nice large window displays a view of rooftops and sky that is sadly slowly filling up with more apartment buildings. Suddenly, space revealed itself differently, essentially. I saw lines of golden threads criss-crossing, spreading, expanding beyond into far spaces. There were layers and interlocking layers—it was endless. It is.

I was awed into stillness, listening to the sound of this unfolding silence, and I knew I was seeing and experiencing the matrix of which we are each a part. I asked for Source to show me more, and more was revealed. I could see further beyond into galaxies. I asked where all this came from—Source showed me a dark hole or space or what seemed like a cave beyond more unnamed galaxies. This matrix of golden strings kept unfolding, spilling out. My whole being tingled with silence, sweetness, wonder. Playfully, I raised my hand and gently pushed on it—the webbed matrix rippled, and I began to see this pattern everywhere in everything.

This led me to know how we are each part of a finely wrought system of strings, interlaced and interconnecting. When I intuit or actually push, ever so gently, against these strings, they move or create a sort of wave that ripples out and away from the point of contact or nudge. The rippling waves continue far and away across distant lands. Everywhere. This led me to think or feel or know or wonder that the quality of that touch that pushes against this enormous web of strings (myself a web within this design) affects the message or the impact on all other receivers of this touch, nudge, push.

This information is not new to people, but what was new to me at the time that I had this experience was the actual seeing of the matrix—strings of intraconnected expanse affected by our thoughts, words and actions.

It is in this matrix that we pulse along from moment to moment interacting in a million ways all at once, synchronistically trying to attain or maintain a balance in our emotional, mental, physical lives. So if this is all true—that we are a complex web of strings in an even more complex web of strings—then it must be right to say, 1) we are all supported–that if we fall, the web of strings will hold us up, and where we are hurt and the strings become broken, they also mend; 2) that we trust the strings that hold us together–for it is a system woven with trust and compassion or whatever emotion/thought we project; 3) that the more conscious whose strings vibrate at finer frequencies and who have integrated such refinement into their own singular web affect this magnificent web with grace.

All our thoughts affect the whole grand design.

So very simple. Why not then live with the awareness of our fine interconnectedness, finer than the music of the finest violin? Why not remember magical moments–sunsets, music, sharing, love-making, excitement of new ideas, et al.–and allow these to re-infuse us with its music? I recalled one particular incident while driving on the freeway. I could see, sense, or feel sensations slowly permeate the layers of my bodybeing, and I became aware of my body as a finely tuned stringed instrument. So elegant, so fine, so poetic. I thought we must consciously choose all our activities–poetry, love-making, eating, talking, walking in the sand so that our minds and hearts be as clear as waters that cleanse and nourish us.

Thought moves our strings; memories do too.

I wondered if we, collectively, sent out at a precise chosen moment a message of love-awareness as a vibration or frequency, then that might create instantly a clear conscious change in all our systems and organizations in all levels of society, starting with our cellular organization. Is this what mystics and sages have been intoning in their practices for eons through their meditations? Is this the poetry of healing?

Is it possible, perhaps, that if we are a web of pulsing and waving strings, that we could look inward and pluck on the strings that have become stuck (thereby causing pain) and release them? That we could undo those aching strings and flush out unwanted dead matter?

Perhaps, this is what holistic practitioners do. Release the dirt caught in tissue and replace cellular consciousness with joyful healthful purpose. Often, raking up the old stuff can leave one more dissatisfied, so there must be a better way out of dark entanglements. Perhaps, clearing the detritus from our cellular memory and reprogramming ourselves is the way. There are healers who are involved in like practices that are both ancient and modern.

After I experienced the vision of our golden matrix, I went for a polarity session with my friend and holistic practitioner, Christel Alkana. During this session of multiple processes—dancing, stretching, sounding, body work—I learned to own my crud and my cleansing process. I believe much magic happened that day. Christel asked me what and how I felt and how we could anchor the new sensibility in my body. I said, "string" and picking on her word "elegant" for my process, I said, "Elegant strings.... I feel like elegant strings...." I was in joy.

When I was ready to leave, Christel dabbed on me some oils. For me she picked the one called Joy. For myself, I picked the one called Forgiveness. These seemed the most appropriate. To be in joyful forgiveness and to know it in my body, for it is a fine intelligence. Too many of us, rushing in our daily routines, seem cut off from this complex receiving, sharing, and transmitting station that the body is–a piece of architectonic wholeness that contains elegantly all life's intricacies.

This dissociation causes complications in our living. We want to be integrated and in resonance. While there are no accidents, there is discernment which may guide our choices, even if they are karmic. And while we experience karmic relationships, we also learn from them and release them. Most of all, we have the choice to awaken our hearts. Someone asked me what language would I like to be fluent in. I said, "the language of the heart." I am still learning. I have a long way to go.

I recall telling my students 10-12 years ago, that if each person picked up a flower at a designated hour across the planet and breathed in its fragrance, there would be, in that instant, a transformation of collective consciousness. Such awakenings are happening more rapidly in our unified field, in our golden matrix. We are still learning and awakening to the fine intelligence of the aware heart—our greater minds.

We are all a part of this matrix of elegant vibrating golden strings. Sometimes we push on them—sometimes we pull on them. This dynamic pattern exists everywhere. It imbues me with a sense of mystery, of wonder, of gratitude.

It is the source of our poetry.

Glossary
For terms and names used in "Continuum—A Love Story"

1. *Chinnamastha:* A form of headless *Kali* that delights in existence and has enormous power as cosmic mind over mind and senses. Also suggests the power of lightning, its indomitable force.

2. *Carvaka:* A materialist philosophy based on logic and skeptical of mystical Hindu beliefs. Pronounced *"chaarvaaka."*

3. *Kali:* Indian goddess of dissolution and destruction. Her purpose is to destroy illusions and maintain divine order; thus, she blesses those that strive for wisdom and divinity. For more information on art relating to Kali, visit — http://www.exoticindiaart.com/kali.htm

4. *Durga:* Indian goddess whose name in sanskrit means invincible. "Du" suggests the 4 evils of poverty, suffering, famine and bad habits. "R" refers to diseases and imbalances, and the "ga" is the destroyer of sins and injustices and evil. Thus, she is the dispeller of darkness and evils.

5. *Santiniketan:* a University established in the town by the same name by 1913 Nobel prize winner Rabindranath Tagore, well-known for his literary accomplishments which include *Gitanjali*.

6. Rabindranath Tagore – see above.

7. *Mahaloka:* Sanskrit word for great beings but suggests location as in a place similar to the Greek Mt. Olympus, a place where reside the great ones. It is a state of consciousness.

9. *Manjusri:* Name of Boddhisattva, one with the power of discrimination or discernment. http://www.buddhanature.com/buddha/manjusri.html

10. *Satyamuni:* "*Satya*" means truth and "*muni*" is a pious person. This name is a referent to Buddha.

11. *Dhruva:* Name for the north star and it means constant one.

References ~

African Legend. "In the Beginning: Bantu Creation Story." *Across Cultures*. Eds. Gillespie and Becker. New York: Longman, 2005

Aguirre, Paul. "Awakened." Collection of student poems. English 102. Cypress College.

Angeles III, Aurelio Gerard C. "To My Dearest Beloved." "I Made You." "The Awakening." *Cascading Suns*. Collection of student poems. English 102. Cypress College. 2004

Blum, Ralph. *The Book of Runes*. New York: St. Martin's Press, 1987

Cage, John. '4'33".' 1952. http://en.wikipedia.org/wiki/John_Cage#4.E2.80.B2_33.E2.80.B3

Cho, Joseph W. "A Sonnet on Perseverance." *Saltwater Taffy*. Collection of student poems. English 102. Cypress College. 2003

Coleridge, Samuel Taylor. "Kubla Khan." http://etext.lib.virginia.edu/stc/Coleridge/poems/Kubla_Khan.html

Duncan, Kathleen. "A Silent Scream." *Saltwater Taffy*. Collection of student poems English 102. Cypress College. 2003

Dung, Vu. "The Orange." "Every Me is Me." *Return to Sacred Waters*. Collection of student poems English 97/English 247. Cypress College. 1997

Hahn, Thich Nhat. *The Heart of Understanding*. Ed. Peter Levitt. Berkeley: Parallax, 1988

Hart, Mickey. *Music to Be Born By*. CD. 360 Degree Productions. 1989

Keats, John. "Ode on a Grecian Urn." http://www.bartleby.com/101/625.html

Kimura, Yasuhiko Genku. "The Third Enlightenment," *The Cosmic Light*, Vol. 2 No. 2, Spring 2000 --Yasuhiko Genku Kimura is founder and chairman of *Vision In Action*. http://www.VIA-VisioninAction.org

Kojiki. Tr. Yasuhiko Genku Kimura. Translated specificallyfor this book by Yasuhiko Genku Kimura, founder and chairman of *Vision In Action*.

Lorde, Audre. "Coping." *Discovering Literature*. Eds. Guth & Rico. New York: Prentice Hall, 2002

Madre De Dios. "Silencio." *O Espiritu de Silencio*. CD

Ngo, Peter P. "Nectarine." "I Am a Mother." *Return to Sacred Waters*. Collection of student poems English 97/English 247. Cypress College. 1997

Olsen, Tillie. "I Stand Here Ironing." *Discovering Literature*. Eds. Guth & Rico. New York: Prentice Hall, 2002

Quiche-Mayan Legend. "Quiche-Mayan Creation Story." *Across Cultures*. Eds. Gillespie & Becker. New York: Longman, 2005

Ratliff, Heather. "Mum." *Cream in Your Coffee*. Collection of student poems, English 97/247. Cypress College. 2003

Rios, Alberto. "Nani." Reprinted by permission of author. First published in *Whispering to Fool the Wind*, copyright Alberto Rios, 1982. Reprinted by permission of the author.

Shakespeare. *Hamlet*. New Haven: Yale UP, 2003

Smith, R.T. "Yonosa House." *Imagining Worlds*. Eds. Ford and Ford. New York: McGraw Hill, 1995

Stanlis, Peter J. Dr. *Address given at Detroit University*. 1962

Stibal, Vianna. *Go Up and Work With God*. Idaho Falls: Rolling Thunder, 2000

Stone, Randolph Dr., "The Wireless Anatomy of Man." *Polarity Therapy*. The Complete Collected Works. Vol. 1 of 2. Sebastopol: SRCS Publications, 1986

The Song of Amergin. http://www.angelfire.com/de2/newconcepts/wicca/amergin.html

"The Universe Within." *NOVA*. PBS. March 7, 1995

Wayman, Tom. "Unemployed." *Waiting for Wayman*. Toronto: McClelland and Stewart, 1973

Wordsworth, William. "I Wandered Lonely as a Cloud." http://www.bartleby.com/145/ww260.html

---

Quotations were found on the site below. References may have changed since my first search and selection.
http://www.gurteen.com/gurteen/gurteen.nsf/(Views)/WebQuoteList?open

About the Author ~

Poet, artist, educator, Ambika Talwar is a Los Angeles transplant, from the historic Indian capital, New Delhi. Her poetry chapbooks published by the Inevitable Press, Laguna Beach, California are titled *Songs of the Body, In the Folds of Your Sari, and Words for Hungry Tongues*. She self-published an earlier collection called *Poems in Color* and continues to be prolific as she travels to new places enjoying new experiences.

Published in *VIA, Inscape* and other journals, she has read at various Southern California venues, in Hawaii and in Paris, France

Winner of the Best Original Story Award for her short film, *Androgyne* in 2000 in Huy, Belgium, she has also developed feature-length scripts, which are held for a future time.

Ambika's work on this book began in the classroom when she had no idea it would bring her to this project. But when she found that students were "getting it" and beginning to enjoy poetry, she decided to bring together the various elements she had used into a cohesive whole. Coming from a holistic perspective, she believes that poetry is about contacting the transcendent self—this inspired students and was effective in helping them overcome their fears.

While Ambika continues to enjoy a successful career as an English instructor at Cypress Community College, near Los Angeles, she is also a holistic healing arts practitioner, particularly theta healing and polarity therapy.

http://www.preciousheartchi.com

Other Works by the Author ~

Print ~

1. *Words for Hungry Tongues*
   This chapbook is a collection of poems published by Inevitable Press of Laguna Beach, California. These poems are explorations of moments of *Eros*, with the idea that all living is *Eros*.

2. *Songs of the Body*
   This chapbook collection of poems explores one's connection with the body and with the mother as the source of language. Also published by Inevitable Press. Limited copies.

3. *In the Folds of Your Sari: Poems for Amma*
   This collection of poems explores her relationship with the divine mother. Written for Mother Karunamayi, the poems are universal and speak of the ubiquitous divine presence, of human longing, and our devotional awakening to the non-dual aspect of divinity.

Film ~

1. *Androgyne*. (29:44) Film written, directed, produced by Ambika Talwar.
   Arista, the protagonist, goes through a crisis with her work believing that all her work is ordinary. Then she makes a masterpiece that magically comes to life and challenges her about her assumptions about life and love. The life-size sculpture named Androgyne desires to be human, and, in her wrangling she threatens Arista. However, only one of them can be human. The film explores the purpose of love and art in our life.
   The film won the **Best Original Story Award** in the **Independent Film** category at the **Festival Mondial du Cinema de Courts Metrages, Belgium**, in 2000 and has shown at other festivals.

Compact Discs ~

2. *Conscious Healing Infusions* – CD
   This CD consists of two powerful visualization meditations and three poetic pieces set to soft music. The meditations lead you through your body to heal imbalances and beliefs. The result is gently powerful, whence the word "infusions."

3. *Dancing with Shiva* – CD
   This CD consists of eroto-spiritual poems set to music by Richard Alexander, composer, currently based in Seattle, Washington.

Information on the above are to be found at the web site – http://www.preciousheartchi.com — E-mail contact is on web site.